ASK DR. ANGELA

Book #701:
Emotional and Physical Abuse
In Relationships,
Part One

Dr. Angela Brownemiller
Dr. Angela®

ASK DR. ANGELA® SERIES
ASK DR. ANGELA About Intimate and Other Partner Abuse and Violence

ASK DR. ANGELA
#701: Emotional and Physical
Abuse in Relationships, Part One

ASK DR. ANGELA

Book #701:
Emotional and Physical Abuse
In Relationships,
Part One

Angela Brownemiller

Metaterra® Publications

ASK DR. ANGELA® SERIES
ASK DR. ANGELA About Intimate and Other Partner Abuse and Violence

<u>Metaterra® Publications</u>
ASK DR. ANGELA
ASK DR. ANGELA SERIES
#701: Emotional and Physical Abuse in Relationships, Part One
Copyright © 2020, 2019, 2013, 2002, 2000, 1998,
Angela Brownemiller/ Angela Browne-Miller.
Copyright © 2020, 2019, 2013, 2002, 2000, 1998, Metaterra® Publications.
Brownemiller, Angela.
1. Psychology. 2. Social Work. 3. Personal Growth.
4. Domestic Violence. 5. Intimate Partner Violence.
6. Violence. 7. Abuse. 8. Addiction.
9. Violence Against Women. 10. Survivors. 11. Batterers.
12. Relationships. 13. Divorce. 14. Self Help.
15. Dr. Angela. 16. Angela Brownemiller. 17. Ask Dr. Angela.
Title:
ASK DR. ANGELA
#701: EMOTIONAL AND PHYSICAL
ABUSE IN RELATIONSHIPS, PART ONE
ISBN-13: 978-1-937951-43-6
Paperback can be ordered on Amazon.com
Ebook and Audiobook forms also see Amazon.com to order.
Published in the United States of America for US and worldwide distribution. Metaterra® Publications.
Book design by and copyright ©Angela Browne-Miller/Angela Brownemiller.
Ordering information and bulk ordering information available through:
Amazon Paperback and Amazon Kindle.
All rights to all printings, formats, and editions reserved. No part of this book (text, graphics, or other) may be reproduced or transmitted in any form or by any means, electronic or mechanical, written, spoken, audio, or other, including photocopying, recording, or by any information storage and retrieval system, etc. without prior written permission from the author, publisher, and copyright owner, except for the inclusion of brief 30 word or shorter quotations in a review. All content, text, graphics as well as cover and interior illustrations, figures, diagrams, have been created by the author, Angela Brownemiller, and cannot be reproduced without her written permission.

ASK DR. ANGELA
#701: Emotional and Physical Abuse in Relationships, Part One

Dedicated to humanity.

ASK DR. ANGELA® SERIES
ASK DR. ANGELA About Intimate and Other Partner Abuse and Violence

ASK DR. ANGELA
#701: Emotional and Physical
Abuse in Relationships, Part One

Note

The information in this book is provided for informational purposes only, without any warranty of any kind. This book is sold and distributed with the understanding that the publisher, the author, and the author's and publisher's consultants, writers, editors, and artists, are not engaged in rendering legal, financial, medical, or other professional services in this book. If legal, financial, medical, or other expert assistance is required, the direct services of a professional should be sought.

ASK DR. ANGELA® SERIES
ASK DR. ANGELA About Intimate and Other Partner Abuse and Violence

ASK DR. ANGELA
#701: Emotional and Physical
Abuse in Relationships, Part One

Table of Contents

Note   7

PART ONE:
GENERAL ASK DR. ANGELA® SERIES
INFORMATION   **11**
Introduction to this ASK DR. ANGELA Series   13
On The Following   17
Hello and Welcome to the
    ASK DR. ANGELA Series   19

PART TWO:
ABOUT THE ASK DR. ANGELA SERIES ON
EMOTIONAL AND
PHYSICAL ABUSE IN RELATIONSHIPS   **21**
Attention Readers   25
On Abuse And Violence In Relationships   27
Note on Stories   35

Note: Readers are encouraged to see the books that come after #701, as this is a series of four books on abuse and violence in relationships:
Ask Dr. Angela #701, Ask Dr. Angela #702,
Ask Dr. Angela #703, and Ask Dr. Angela #704.
See Amazon.com and also DrAngela.com
for more information.

PART THREE
WELCOME TO ASK DR. ANGELA, BOOK #701   **37**
1. Introduction To Book #701   41
2. For Knowing No Harm   43

ASK DR. ANGELA® SERIES
ASK DR. ANGELA About Intimate and Other Partner Abuse and Violence

3. The Lifetime Of Effects	51
4. Last Time Story	*67*
5. All About Intentions	69
6. What About Consent	95
7. Power Difference Story	*101*
8. Precious Time	105
9. Cherish is a Word For	113
10. Second Thought Story	*127*
11. Individual Identity and Boundaries Within a Relationship	129
12. Meet the IP's Boundary	137
13. Anatomy of the Bond	147
14. Messages Story	*155*
15. Signs	157
16. Any Idea Story	*173*
17. Denial?	175
18. What Strength Story	*179*
19. Emotional Abuse Itself, And Emotional Abuse Against The Backdrop Of Threatened Or Actual Physical Abuse	181

NOW SEE
    THE NEXT BOOK IN THIS SERIES, #702 — **191**

APPENDICES — **193**
Booklist and Recommended Reading — 195
About The Real Ask Dr. Angela® — 197
About the Author — 199
Seeing the Hidden Face of Addiction (Book) — 201
Navigating Life's Stuff (Book) — 203
The ASK DR. ANGELA SERIES (Books, etc.) — 204

ASK DR. ANGELA
#701: Emotional and Physical
Abuse in Relationships, Part One

PART ONE
GENERAL
ASK DR. ANGELA® SERIES
INFORMATION

The following section of this book is placed at the opening of all ASK DR. ANGELA books, and presents this overview of the
ASK DR. ANGELA SERIES of
Books, Ebooks, Audiobooks, and
Podcasts, Broadcasts,
Columns, Articles, Workshops, Sessions,
And other events and services.

The chapters in this general section include:
• Introduction To This Ask Dr. Angela® Series
• Just Ask Dr. Angela®
• Hello and Welcome To The Ask Dr. Angela® Series

Following this general section, we move into
PART TWO, which is specifically regarding the
ASK DR. ANGELA Series on
Emotional and Physical Abuse in Relationships.

ASK DR. ANGELA® SERIES
ASK DR. ANGELA About Intimate and Other Partner Abuse and Violence

ASK DR. ANGELA
#701: Emotional and Physical
Abuse in Relationships, Part One

Introduction To This
ASK DR. ANGELA SERIES

****

Do you control your brain, your mind, or does it control you? Are you in charge of how you feel, what you think, and what you do? Or is something else really running us? Do we know? How do we know? And does it make a difference, in our lives, in our daily lives, in our moment to moment feelings of wellness, happiness, success, optimism, whatever these feelings might be.

Just ASK DR. ANGELA ® for her views on all this….

****

Meet the ASK DR. ANGELA® Series of books/Ebooks, audiobooks, podcasts, broadcasts, workshops, programs, services, consults, and events. Here, Dr. Angela®, also known as Dr. Angela Brownemiller, talks about us, we humans, who we are, what we are, and perhaps even why we are. The big and the small questions, major and minor issues in our lives, are all important as these affect us on some level at all times. As Dr. Angela always says:

EVERY MOMENT MATTERS.

What makes us think, feel, and behave the way we do? If we wish to enjoy, expand upon, or even adjust or change a little or

ASK DR. ANGELA® SERIES
ASK DR. ANGELA About Intimate and Other Partner Abuse and Violence

a lot of what we are thinking, feeling, and doing, how can we do this in healthy ways? Are we such creatures of habit that we are ever tied to the emotional, behavioral, and thought patterns we form?

Can we change, shift, even leave these patterns if we wish to? Dr. Angela says, yes we can NAVIGATE LIFE'S STUFF. (See other books by Dr. Angela, some of which are actually titled, *NAVIGATING LIFE'S STUFF*).

This ASK DR. ANGELA Series is about you, about whatever you feel is something you might be asking, about your life, your mind, your brain, your body – your spirit, your SELF. A range of topics are covered in the *ASK DR. ANGELA Series Books*.

The *ASK DR. ANGELA Series Books* offer information, insights, and answers to questions many people have asked Dr. Angela as part of the ASK DR. ANGELA projects and programs. The *ASK DR. ANGELA Books* answer and expand upon these questions, drawing from publications and recordings where Dr. Angela Brownemiller answers in person, and also in various podcasts, broadcasts, speeches, workshops, consulting sessions, and other message forms such as her extensive books on social, psychological, consciousness, well-being, health and wellness, and other issues.

Some of these *ASK DR. ANGELA Books* address abuse and violence in relationships. (These particular books are numbered *#701, #702, #703, #704* – the book here on the following pages is *#701*).

ASK DR. ANGELA
#701: Emotional and Physical Abuse in Relationships, Part One

This particular book, *#701*, is the first in, and foundation of, this series which focuses on this special area of interest and concern of many people out there: emotional and even physical abuse and violence in intimate partner relationships. The title of this book is therefore:

ASK DR. ANGELA
Book #701:
Emotional and Physical Abuse In Relationships,
Part **One**

See also these other books by Dr. Angela, addressing other aspects of abuse and violence in relationships:

ASK DR. ANGELA
Book #702:
Emotional and Physical Abuse In Relationships,
Part **Two**
(This #702 book follows #701.)

ASK DR. ANGELA
Book #703:
Emotional and Physical Abuse In Relationships,
Part **Three**
(This #703 book follows #702.)

ASK DR. ANGELA
Book #704:
Emotional and Physical Abuse In Relationships,
Part **Four**
(This #704 book follows #703.)

ASK DR. ANGELA® SERIES
ASK DR. ANGELA About Intimate and Other Partner
Abuse and Violence

ASK DR. ANGELA
#701: Emotional and Physical Abuse in Relationships, Part One

On The Following

Please note that the following is itself not therapy or other forms of treatment. If you are experiencing states of mind or body that are affecting your mental and or physical health and well-being, please contact a professional mental or physical health expert right away. While Dr. Brownemiller is an expert, she does neither diagnoses nor treats people from the pages of her books or the sound waves of her shows. Thank you.

ASK DR. ANGELA® SERIES
ASK DR. ANGELA About Intimate and Other Partner Abuse and Violence

ASK DR. ANGELA
#701: Emotional and Physical Abuse in Relationships, Part One

HELLO AND WELCOME TO THE ASK DR. ANGELA SERIES

Hello and Welcome. This is Dr. Angela® with answers to and comments on the ASK DR. ANGELA questions and comments you have sent me. Many of you have asked from where it is that I am speaking to you. Let me note that this varies, and is best described as everywhere you find me – in person, in books, Ebooks, audiobooks, and or online, on ground, via airwaves, and beyond.

Sure, there are those of you who tell me you feel so connected you hear me speaking to you when you are alone and or when you are recalling information and advice I may have shared. Your sense of your own level of intuitive communication or connection, I leave to you to define.

And yes, for those of you who wish this confirmed, I am here writing to you on planet Earth.

As you know, I, in the books, podcasts, and programs in this *ASK DR. ANGELA ® SERIES*, talk about us, all of us, and therefore also about you, your mind, your mind/brain, your behaviors, your life, your feelings, your relationships, and more.

ASK DR. ANGELA® SERIES
ASK DR. ANGELA About Intimate and Other Partner
Abuse and Violence

Remember, the life you save may be your own...

and others' lives too....

Dr. Angela®

PART TWO

ABOUT THE

ASK
DR. ANGELA
SERIES ON

Emotional and Physical Abuse In Relationships

(Books #701, #702, #703, #704)

The chapters in this PART TWO section include:
- Attention Readers
- About Abuse and Violence in Relationships
- Note on Stories

Following this PART TWO section of this book,
we then move into
PART THREE of this book, which is the main content of
Book #701, the first book in this four book
ASK DR. ANGELA SERIES
on Abuse and Violence in Relationships.

ASK DR. ANGELA® SERIES
ASK DR. ANGELA About Intimate and Other Partner
Abuse and Violence

ASK DR. ANGELA
#701: Emotional and Physical Abuse in Relationships, Part One

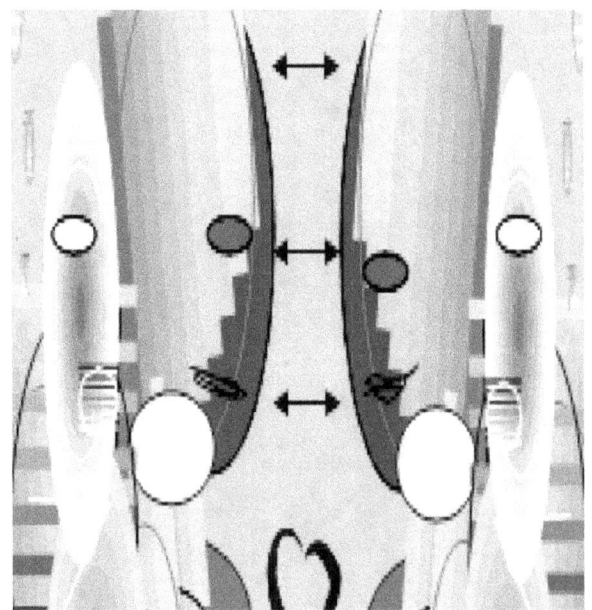

On Micro-Relating
Illustration by Angela Brownemiller

*I've been abused so long
it looks like love to me.*

ASK DR. ANGELA® SERIES
ASK DR. ANGELA About Intimate and Other Partner Abuse and Violence

ASK DR. ANGELA
#701: Emotional and Physical
Abuse in Relationships, Part One

Attention Readers

This book is intended to offer readers insight into healthy and less than healthy—troubled, unsafe, sometimes even quite dangerous—interactions taking place in intimate (and other) partner relationships. Many readers will arrive here, on these pages, once someone—either they themselves, or their family members, friends, neighbors, co-workers, therapists, health care providers, faith leaders, law enforcement and court officials, colleagues, or others—have brought them here.

Of course, where there is a clear, and sometimes less than clear, yet relatively or possibly immediate or imminent danger to self or others, these words in this book can wait, and every step to ensure immediate safety must be taken right away. Emergency hot lines, police lines, shelter lines, doctors' numbers, and other contact information must be used to seek and attain information regarding safety and protection.

This book is written for use where there is room and time for reflection and thought, for an increase in awareness regarding what is actually taking place, or has actually already taken place, in healthy relating, yes—and also in possible and actual abusive and violent interactions between partners. So often, we are too caught up (in what we feel) to see in some detail what is taking place in close interpersonal relationships, and to note where there is the potential for any form of abuse and violence—or where there already is abuse and violence underway. Many of us are therefore at times prone to miss signs of nonphysical abuse and even of potentially dangerous physical violence brewing, to only see these after the fact.

ASK DR. ANGELA® SERIES
ASK DR. ANGELA About Intimate and Other Partner Abuse and Violence

Also note that this book is written for adults over the age of eighteen, however much of the discussion on interactions herein is also relevant to teens in relationship, dating, and or other emotional and physical intimacy situations. Readers who are underage, or who are providing this book to someone underage, will please also ensure that young people have adult involvement in understanding and using this material.

ASK DR. ANGELA
#701: Emotional and Physical Abuse in Relationships, Part One

ON ABUSE AND VIOLENCE IN RELATIONSHIPS

Virtually every day we hear of ongoing and new incidents of abuse, violence, and even terror, in homes, schools, workplaces, and elsewhere in our communities and in our nations around the globe.

Among these instances are those that too often take place at one of the most interpersonal levels, in the relationship between domestic, marital, dating, intimate, and or other forms of partners connected and sometimes bound by love, law, tradition, and or other personal partnering practices such as sexual intimacy.

TO FURTHER RAISE AWARENESS

What is ever more clear is that people, causes, professions, services, laws, policies, traditions, sometimes even religious practices, tend to not understand, or to not recognize, or fail to see, refuse to address, consider less important, or even do not accept, the full range of violence and abuse within personal (such as dating, love, partner, spousal, and other) relationships.

This series of books, *ASK DR. ANGELA #701, ASK DR. ANGELA #702, ASK DR. ANGELA #703,* and *ASK DR. ANGELA #704,* seeks to help raise awareness of problems that can arise in human relationships, especially in intimate partner, marital, dating, and similar relationships.

ASK DR. ANGELA® SERIES
ASK DR. ANGELA About Intimate and Other Partner Abuse and Violence

This book moves the discussion of intimate and other partner violence and abuse to a place the discussion may not visit enough, to the most basic locus of relating, the frequently quite subtle interpersonal communication, interaction, and even moment to moment, *micro-interaction*, levels.

CALLING FOR A
FAR CLOSER LOOK

Much of today's excellent work and research on intimate partner abuse and violence overlooks this finer unit of analysis, the minute to minute, second to second, micro levels of interpersonal interaction. Yet, it is in the moment to moment interactions themselves that the *dynamics of abuse, and even of the steps into all out physical violence*, appear, sometimes quite subtly, yet often clearly if we know what to look for.

Hence, this book draws our focus away from some of the more general concepts and issues, to an ever more critical and intricate level of interpersonal interaction.

HIDDEN AND
SUBTLE LEVELS OF ABUSE

This level is where spoken words, as well as frequently quite subtle and hidden, spoken perhaps yet oft unspoken communications, compromises, trades—implicit and explicit, informal and formal, imagined and real—various kept, altered, and broken tendencies, arrangements and

ASK DR. ANGELA
#701: Emotional and Physical Abuse in Relationships, Part One

agreements—are underway at all times.[1]

There is so much to see in interactions between partners, so much so very wonderful. And yes, there is sometimes (in some, but not all relationships) a great deal to see that is problematic (and or *potentially* problematic)—even at times dangerous emotionally, physically, and in other ways such as socially, economically, financially, professionally, and so on.

And there is also so much more to become aware of even when at first it is difficult to see. Indeed, there is so much abuse and violence that is difficult to see because it is difficult to define, or confusing, or quite subtle, or even purposefully hidden for various reasons.

INTIMACY?

Therefore this book is written for anyone who will sometime be in, is presently in, and or is looking back upon a previous, intimate partner "and or" love, dating, or other similar form of relationship.

I write "and or" as not all intimate (and or other) partner relationships are "love" relationships—and vice versa. While these two conditions—love and intimate partnership—frequently occur together, it is all too common that we find people in intimate partner relationships who think there is love

---

[1] Note: In other books, I, Dr. Angela, offer still finer units of analysis such as the brain cell, synaptic, biochemical, and neuro-transmitter levels of all this. See the four volume set on *VIOLENCE AND ABUSE IN SOCIETY*, editor Angela Brownemiller (Browne-Miller). See also other books by this author as per recommended reading listed at the end of this present book.

there, when there may or may not be love—or when the love may or may not be what the love is assumed to be or mean.

Additionally, there is a great deal of confusion regarding intimacy. We must ask: does intimacy guarantee anything—love, stability, safety, truth, clarity, or …? What troubled illusions might moments of emotional and physical intimacy without true caring, commitment, and awareness sometimes foster? Should we wonder?

And of course, intimacy itself varies in definition and nature across relationships, with physical intimacy being only one level of intimacy that can occur in relationships.

THIS BOOK IS WRITTEN FOR EVERYONE

This book is written for everyone who may at some time be in or around a relationship. This means that this book is also written for others—family members, friends, neighbors, coworkers, helping and health professionals—who are seeing and perhaps working to address the needs of spouses and partners in relationships that are working well and in relationships that are troubled or may be troubled.

An additional note….

LOOKING BEYOND DEBATES

Various and frequently heated debates have arisen regarding the acceptability of, existence of, nature of, and solutions to, violence and abuse in relationships. Interestingly, these debates vary and even differ significantly among different belief system and cultural groups, as well as among

ASK DR. ANGELA
#701: Emotional and Physical Abuse in Relationships, Part One

professions and professional perspectives, and communities, regions, and nations of the world.

Too often, one is forced to "take a side" in these debates, to accept a view or theory prior to looking quite closely at the most subtle and micro levels of relating.

While it is not the intent of this book to take a position on most of these overarching debates, certain realities will be acknowledged here, already on these first pages. Let me begin by making it clear that neither the perpetration nor the receiving of violence and abuse is restricted to one gender (or to one sexual preference for that matter).

PEOPLE FREQUENTLY ABUSE PEOPLE

Men can and do abuse women and men, and women can and do abuse men and women. This reality warrants earnest and honest attention. This book, which focuses on interactions between people who are in relationships, attempts to distill interpersonal relationship abuse down to relatively gender-neutral processes.

Yet, despite the reality that both genders can and do experience violence and abuse in relationships, there is another matter that warrants equal concern here:

WOMEN AND GIRLS

Abuse of and violence against women and girls is a longtime issue, even tradition, of worldwide significance, something that has continued to exist at crisis levels around the globe.

ASK DR. ANGELA® SERIES
ASK DR. ANGELA About Intimate and Other Partner Abuse and Violence

Indeed, one of the signal issues of our times is how to stop violence against women and girls. So much of this violence has been taking place throughout history, and has been virtually institutionalized for centuries.

Indeed, over the centuries women were the property or chattel of men in many societies, and where not, nevertheless lived with fewer rights to property and decisions and even freedom than men did, and in some places than men still do.

Descending from this long tradition of seconding women to their fathers, brothers, husbands, and others in their lives, we see even today that abuse and violence against women quite frequently falls into this domain.

*Even where women and girls are no longer treated as second class citizens, there can and do remain both obvious and **hidden traces** of such perspectives.*

*We must remain **ever watchful** for these. In instances where even these traces do remain, any and all of the possibilities of violence and abuse against, and even terrorizing of, women and girls, can be perpetuated in some way, even magnified or enhanced when and where we least expect this.*

Even where age old forms of violence and abuse of women may appear to be receding, new and powerful yet subtle even hidden forms may be emerging.

We must do everything we can to stop this long term, even age old, frequently approved or at least tolerated socially, abuse of and violence against women and girls taking place around the world, to stop the femicide, infanticide, trapping and

ASK DR. ANGELA
#701: Emotional and Physical Abuse in Relationships, Part One

trafficking, maiming, beating, terrorizing, and the socially, verbally, financially, and other definitely abusive behaviors taking place.

FINE TUNING
OUR ATTENTION TO ALL FORMS

Ultimately, it is essential we are always fine tuning our policies, attitudes, and awarenesses regarding violence and abuse against people by people—*no matter who they are, where they are, what their age, what their gender*—this is essential.

This book offers one contribution to the major peace promoting efforts of our times.

ASK DR. ANGELA® SERIES
ASK DR. ANGELA About Intimate and Other Partner Abuse and Violence

ASK DR. ANGELA
#701: Emotional and Physical
Abuse in Relationships, Part One

Note on Stories

Several scenarios, labeled herein as "stories," are placed throughout this book as examples of intimate partner abuse and violence, and related relationship conditions and their effects. Some of these stories are rather graphic depictions of violence and abuse, and others may seem to some readers to be comparatively innocuous, relatively harmless along a spectrum of degrees of harm and danger. Yet, each story contains within it at least one element of, or potential precursor to, abuse and violence, usually several. And no matter how minor these elements may seem, they can be representative of larger problems.

Also, even the seemingly most harmless abuse events may be signs of other current or emerging abuses that may be still more serious, or that may be increasingly harmful in their accumulation, and should be given attention.

The stories included herein are based upon, composed by combining, hundreds of actual persons' stories. These actual persons exist in a range of sociocultural settings; however, herein all their names, settings, and identifying factors have been changed to protect identities. In some cases but not all, genders have been made impossible to know and or no names have been given. Where gender has been indicated or suggested, this is done with the understanding that gender may be changed for each character in each story.

Any resemblance to particular persons living or dead is unintentional and is the product of the possible commonality of these experiences across gender, race, cultural, socioeconomic, and other

ASK DR. ANGELA® SERIES
ASK DR. ANGELA About Intimate and Other Partner Abuse and Violence

groups. Also note that where the names may have been changed to names more typical of some gender and or cultural groups than others, this is not in itself an indication that any particular group experiences these situations more than any other. Readers are invited to substitute for others whatever names and genders they wish as they read along.

Although many of these stories are not happy stories, most of the stories included here stop at their own midpoints for instructional reasons. This is not to paint an unhealed or ugly picture of love or relationships. This is to allow readers to observe potential and actual problems in relationships, in the interactions, the agreements, the behaviors, and in the issues that must be seen, recognized, addressed, to be changed.

In fact, many of the real stories upon which this book is based have ended well for their participants in their own learning, healing, change, transformation—either within or beyond these relationships. Another book, another time, with another purpose, can tell these other stories.

Clearly, countless other stories could have been included had space permitted. Most readers will have at least one story of their own. We all know relationship stories that are relevant to the following discussion of what hurts and what works. More likely than not, we ourselves have experienced directly, or witnessed directly, some of these stories and understand these from the inside.

PART THREE

Welcome To

ASK
DR. ANGELA

Book #701:
Emotional and Physical Abuse
In Relationships,
Part One

ASK DR. ANGELA® SERIES
ASK DR. ANGELA About Intimate and Other Partner Abuse and Violence

ASK DR. ANGELA
#701: Emotional and Physical
Abuse in Relationships, Part One

Again, note that the following is itself not therapy or other forms of treatment. If you are experiencing states of mind or body that are affecting your mental and or physical health and well-being, please contact a professional mental or physical health expert right away. While Dr. Brownemiller is an expert, she does neither diagnoses nor treats people from the pages of her books or the sounds waves of her shows. Thank you.

**ASK DR. ANGELA® SERIES
ASK DR. ANGELA About Intimate and Other Partner
Abuse and Violence**

ASK DR. ANGELA
#701: Emotional and Physical
Abuse in Relationships, Part One

Chapter 1
Introduction to Book #701

Before beginning here, I want to acknowledge the great amount of work that has been done in this field. So much has been said and done about domestic violence and intimate partner violence. Research has been conducted, legislation has been written, laws have been enforced, restraining orders have been implemented, arrests have been made, courts have ruled, programs for both the survivors and the perpetrators and have been developed, and more.

And still there is continuing occurrence of abuse and violence (and even in some cases terror) in intimate partner, spousal, unmarried significant other, dating, casual, and other forms of interpersonal relationships. The complexities of this abuse and violence are still being learned about, and are addressed in this series of books (*ASK DR. ANGELA #701, #702, #703, and #704*).

Indeed abuse itself is violence, is a violation of a boundary. And indeed abuse itself takes many forms, some minor and some marked, some even quite treacherous. What is most concerning is that nonviolent, emotional abuse, is frequently the precursor to, or even cover for, physical violence also taking place. And, all too often, emotional and verbal abuse are used as an excuse for physical violence. (For example, we all too frequently hear troubling excuses such as this: "She wouldn't shut up, so I hit her. She responded by crying and spitting in my face, so I punched

ASK DR. ANGELA® SERIES
ASK DR. ANGELA About Intimate and Other Partner Abuse and Violence

her and knocked her tooth out. If she had just shut up, none of this would have happened. It's her fault.")

Additionally, the long term effects of intimate partner abuse and violence are barely recognized. These effects span physical and mental health, as well as social and even financial health. And rarely is the perpetrator of past partner violence available to admit let alone address and help with the long term effects of that violence that took place decades later.

Few out there who were frequently physically beaten during marriages or relationships that were in place earlier in their lives arrive at middle age and senior age unaffected. There is an absolute long term affect that is barely addressed. Certainly, there are more long term medical studies surfacing. These are indeed indicating that the long term health effects of intimate partner violence appear to be significantly more serious in women than in men. This warrants further research and great concern.

Far too many women reaching the ages of 50, 60, 70, and beyond, are experiencing the now surfacing long term health consequences of being beaten by an intimate partner years, even decades, earlier. How will we as a society come to terms with this long range and generally disregarded outcome?

Let's begin by fine tuning our awareness of the complexities of abuse and violence on the following pages….

The Author
Dr Angela Brownemiller

ASK DR. ANGELA
#701: Emotional and Physical
Abuse in Relationships, Part One

Chapter 2
For Knowing No Harm

If these pages could cry, they would shed oceans of tears for those suffering the pain, anguish, confusion, and humiliation of intimate partner abuse and violence. These tears would be for the persons being abused, for the persons who are doing the abusing, and for their children, parents, other family members, friends, neighbors, coworkers, communities, societies, and worlds. Whether or not we choose to acknowledge this, we all feel the shattering of the hearts, minds, souls, and even bodies of people whose lives are or have at some time been infected with intimate partner abuse in its various physical and nonphysical forms.

A word about the person who is abusing—frequently described as the abuser, batterer, or perpetrator....

Do not think every person abusing is free of the pain, anguish, confusion, and humiliation experienced by the persons being abused. Many of them have themselves been abused or witnessed abuse and violence in earlier situations, frequently as children. And or they have been conditioned to believe that their abuses, or the abuses they are pressured psychologically or socially to perform, are not abuses, or are acceptable and even sometimes required abuses. And, whether or not this is the case, they will have to live (either consciously or subconsciously or both) with the experience of harming others, hurting people, and beating on the bodies and hearts of people they likely love or once loved, or said they loved, for the rest of their lives.

What it takes for these persons to stand up and be counted, to own the behaviors of harm in which they have engaged, and then to change, is immense. Whether standing up to family, social, cultural, traditional, religious, or personal impulses and norms pressing them to abuse, they themselves may face external and internal reprisals that are rarely talked about or acknowledged.

Clearing the legacy of inflicting harm, and lighting the way for others to follow this path, is key to moving past the history of harm and to helping create a world which might someday be free of interpersonal harm.

And a word about the person being abused—frequently described as the *abusee* in this book, also known as the survivor, or the victim. We do know that many persons who have been abused by their intimate partners have been so very deeply affected that they will be dealing with the social, economic, professional, mental, spiritual, and physical effects for the rest of their lives.

For these persons, identifying and then healing and moving past the wounds is a large job, which first requires deep commitment to oneself and then to the people one loves. *(Note again that even moving past the wounds does not necessarily eliminate all traces of these, as many wounds remain for a lifetime.)*

Standing up and being counted, owning the experience, and then owning the recovery process, are all essential. We need to know what human beings are capable of doing to other

ASK DR. ANGELA
#701: Emotional and Physical Abuse in Relationships, Part One

human beings. We need to know that human beings can sometimes cause, even the people closest to them, often their intimate partners, great harm.

Clearing the legacy of being harmed, and lighting the way for others to follow this path, is key to moving past the history of being harmed and to helping create a world which might someday be free of interpersonal harm.

Each and every one of us is a benefactor and a victim of the human condition. We are living in a world which tolerates and even sometimes glorifies violence as a means of resolving disputes, disagreements, tensions. Just look at the world today, or just see the internet or watch the television.

We have all arrived at this time in history together, facing the pressure to evolve to a higher point of consciousness or to remain a violent species, treating humans violently, treating life violently, treating the Earth violently.

What a wonderful place in which to respond to this survival pressure and to help raise consciousness—a close intimate partner relationship with another being!

If these pages can contribute even a little to the evolution of this consciousness, they will. In fact, these pages seek to offer suggestions for:

- getting to better know oneself and oneself in relationship.
- increasing understanding of what takes place in intimate partner, significant other, dating, casual, and other sorts of relationships.

- raising the consciousness of intimate partners with the goal of reaching highly conscious relating.
- stopping the violence and abuse in relationships by openly and clearly recognizing it for what it is, and…
   - by changing it where it can be changed, or if necessary,
   - by knowing when to get out of it,
      - away from it for a time
      - or for good.

Stopping the clock to look closely at what is taking place when we interact, freeze-framing the process we are partaking in, can allow us to understand close up and personally **the intricate workings** *of the energies of two people engaged in pleasure and or harm to themselves and others.* **The dances people in relationships do are highly elaborate, quite interactive, and more readily understood in very slow motion.**

IPAVT IS COMPLEX

This book looks closely at intimate partner violence, also known as **IPV**, to define its intricacies in greater depth. Intimate partner abuse, violence, and terror (what this book defines as **IPAV, IPAVT** and **IPAV&T**) is truly complex. *Popular but limited single-theory explanations for these problems say very little about what is actually taking place.*

The various competing socio-political schools of thought regarding intimate partner abuse and violence do best by ceasing the competition and seeing the multitude of factors at

ASK DR. ANGELA
#701: Emotional and Physical
Abuse in Relationships, Part One

work. Reality is not simple, and is not merely a very general or broad social system level issue. So why would we expect relationships or relationship violences to be simple?

Some people spend entire lifetimes mired in very difficult relationships and or the aftermaths of these. For many of them, these problem relationship behaviors become habitual, increasingly difficult, and sometimes even dangerous to break away from without guidance and assistance.

What does it take to leave behind the patterns of denial, confusion, wounds, pain, sadness, and agony? Seeing and changing one's experience of it all is quite health-promoting, even essential. Owning one's role does not mean voluntarily wearing for life a label such as abus__ee__ or abus__er__, survivor or batterer, and victim or perpetrator.

Labels are only labels and not who we are. (*The exception here might be in cases where perpetrators who are highly likely to perpetrate again, perhaps in new relationships, wear these labels to protect others who might become their next victims. Debate regarding this matter is left for other books.*)

Wearing these labels while working to understand and change them, or to leave them behind, is useful. Getting past these labels into entirely new roles and identities is not only moving on, not only healing, but also healthy living.

So, yes, identify one's own relationship to such labels, identify with such labels, as long as this helps to understand what has happened and to heal. Let no one take this process away. Then, when ready and able, move past these labels. For example, if one is a survivor of domestic violence, see this, know this, and deal with this—wear the label as long as it takes to understand this experience, and then move on to new understandings of self and be proud of this progress.

CONSCIOUS RELATIONSHIPS

In the end, the goal here is to help enlighten us regarding what can take place in intimate partner and love relationships, and where even happy and high functioning patterns of relating can sometimes run into trouble.

Through the process of examining our own and others' behaviors in relationships, and the ways that we can change our behaviors related to these relationships, we can raise the consciousness of ourselves, of our relationships, of the world around us, and of our children who very much need to see healthy relationships, healthy looking at problems within relationships, and intelligent, aware responses to social, psychological, biological, and biochemical drives.

We *can* enter and maintain conscious relationships in which we do conscious relating to ourselves and each other. *This does not mean that we need endless hours processing and reprocessing infinite aspects of each and every detail and element of our relationships.*

This does mean that we *consciously choose* to be involved *consciously*, to know what goes on in relationships, what healthy and unhealthy interactions may look like, what unspoken and spoken contracts and promises we may make, what various warning signs are, and what it takes to keep

ASK DR. ANGELA
#701: Emotional and Physical
Abuse in Relationships, Part One

ourselves conscious of what we are doing with each other and ourselves.

CONSCIOUS RELATING TO OUR LOVED ONES AND OURSELVES

This book seeks to focus in on the process of *conscious relating*, on what it takes to be more aware of the often invisible *subtle levels of interactions* taking place within interpersonal relationships. Conscious relating to these interactions requires close attention to both the spoken and the unspoken agreements and contracts we make with our intimate partners, and close attention to the relationship between our own subconscious and our own consciousness.

In the end, we are responsible for learning how to know and then knowing ourselves, and for managing our responses to what life has dealt us. The responsibility for recognizing, changing, overcoming, and or safely leaving intimate partner abuse and violence is upon us.

This book encourages a deep and honest look at the specific interactions, and energy exchanges, taking place in our intimate partner relationships, as this is the first and biggest step in recognizing and changing these relationships.

Each individual interaction on this planet mirrors a piece of the whole human story. Each interaction reflects in daily life a piece of the greater human strife and joy on this Earth. As large as the world's population is, it is made up of billions and billions of individual people in billions of interpersonal

ASK DR. ANGELA® SERIES
ASK DR. ANGELA About Intimate and Other Partner Abuse and Violence

and intimate partner relationships, engaging in and often struggling with billions of dynamics, including billions of aspects of love and caring, and also billions of little and big physical and nonphysical abuses and violences against others and toward selves taking place each day, at least some of which are touched upon in this book.

Let's say for a moment that violence is cumulative and that all violence affects all humanity. Say that on some level, even if we prefer not to, even if we do not realize we are, we sense, feel, and hear pain of violence coming from the other side of the world. Then, any amount of violence hurts us all. Then, any amount of violence—even the slightest and most invisible—which we ourselves can put a stop to, we must stop.

Clearly there is a great deal of violence in this world. This book seeks to help bring about at least a momentary "aha"— to inspire a bit of hookup—to connect us to the larger picture. We can attune ourselves to, feel the link between, our personal and interpersonal behaviors, and those of the whole of humanity, and even of the whole of life on Earth. To achieve this sense of connection is a lofty goal, and readers are asked to contribute to this process, join in connecting the dots.

We can create a wave of change by starting at home, in our own interpersonal relations, modeling intelligent alternatives to abuse and violence. And it is never too late to begin the process of nonviolent relating. Any attention to this process which any one can give and share is much needed in this world.

ASK DR. ANGELA
#701: Emotional and Physical
Abuse in Relationships, Part One

Chapter 3
The Lifetime Of Effects

Many partner, marriage, and dating relationships are truly absolutely wonderful. Many other relationships are indeed at least quite pleasant, quite worthwhile, handle the realities of life quite functionally, and adapt successfully to most changes and challenges.

Other relationships are less functional, perhaps somewhat functional yet emotionally and or physically distressing, some unsafe, even abusive. Some other relationships are definitely emotionally and or physically brutal.

Emotionally and physically abusive and brutal relationship experiences are complex. And they are riddled with difficult to recognize precursors, triggers, characteristics, motivations, and often with co-occurring issues.

The effects of troubled relationship experiences can last for a lifetime, sometimes even lifetimes when children and others around the relating are affected and the effects carry into generations. Frequently the abuse in relationships continues for far too long, sometimes throughout the life of the relationship itself, and sometimes even after the relationship has ended.

Too many people are dealing with very difficult relationship experiences on an ongoing basis, their pain frequently hidden (hidden from others as well as from themselves).

ASK DR. ANGELA® SERIES
ASK DR. ANGELA About Intimate and Other Partner Abuse and Violence

The love relationship can and usually does bring great comfort, meaning, closeness, tenderness, identity, and many other positive aspects to life. For many, a loving relationship can be central in life, and can become a beautiful and fulfilling way of life.

However, the troubled relationship, which may or may not look like love to one or more members of the relationship, or to onlookers, can also become a way of life in itself. The troubled relationship tends to seek to sustain itself, to do what it takes to dominate processes and lives.

Many times, the drive of the troubled relationship to sustain itself as it is, as troubled, continues undetected.

In fact, many troubled relationships manage to look like good relationships, or at least "alright relationships." When we are caught in a troubled relationship, and have been caught for a while, we may adapt to it. We think things are "not so bad," "nothing to worry about," maybe even "worth it." Or we may feel we have no other option.

We think we feel the deep sorrow less and less over time. This adaptation to a troubled relationship is both an individual adaptation and a relationship adaptation. Quite often, this is also a whole family adaptation.

We think we have adapted to it, we think we feel the deep sorrow less. Oh, but we feel it, oh how we feel it. We, either consciously or subconsciously, try to bury awareness of the distress so deeply that we can pretend it is not right before us, there with us every single waking and sleeping moment. We avoid drawing our attention to what is really taking

ASK DR. ANGELA
#701: Emotional and Physical Abuse in Relationships, Part One

place, avoid asking the questions that might bring answers and awareness—and even safety.

Victims of, and perpetrators of, what this book is defining as IPAVT are known to sometimes even avoid seeing bruises and cuts right before their eyes, sometimes even broken bones, avoiding admitting realities that are actually quite easy to see the source of under most conditions.

**Do we really believe we are
truly ignoring what is truly going on?
No.
Are we able to see or sense on a deep level
what is actually going on?
Yes.
Are there questions we indeed should be asking,
yet avoid asking...
<u>to avoid having to address</u>
the violence and abuse taking place?
Sometimes yes.**

INTIMATE PARTNER VIOLENCE IS PREVALENT

Troubled intimate partner relationships can indeed hurt. In fact, in terms of actual physical pain, intimate partner violence results in millions of injuries and deaths around the world each year. And this is before adding on data estimates for countless unreported incidents as well as data for events not typically included in standard IPV definitions *(standard intimate partner violence by formal definitions not including the expanded range of IPAVT defined in this book)*--such as types of partner rape and some other forms of sexual assault, and a range of physical and nonphysical abuses and terrors also not considered standard IPV. These are not always considered events taking place between "intimate" "partners," and or not considered wrong enough, or violent enough to be classed as violent—and therefore these events are quite frequently not counted in standard IPV data. (Note here: As will be emphasized in the last chapter of this book, emotional abuse itself can be painful, harmful, dangerous, damaging, and is even in itself a form of VIO-lence.)

Ultimately, given abused persons' general reluctance to report the abuse and violence, what the official data do say are vast understatements. Also note that persons, especially women, who have separated from their abusive partners often remain at risk of violence, sometimes even increased risk. However, much of this post partnership risk and perpetration data is not collected. Moreover, victims of violence and threatened violence repeated over time experience more serious short- and long term consequences than victims of one-time incidents and threats, yet these data tend not to be counted.

INCLUDES NONPHYSICAL FORMS

The "hurt" we are talking about has many dimensions. These dimensions also do include nonphysical types of abuse and violence which can be precursors to physical violence, or can be extremely hurtful, miserable, and destructive even in the absence of physical violence.

ASK DR. ANGELA
#701: Emotional and Physical Abuse in Relationships, Part One

These nonphysical forms of violence are common yet easily mislabeled and can be missed altogether. *For example, threatened violence especially when ongoing, is abuse, and is violence in itself, and is terrorizing.*

Whether threatened violence or another form of abuse, emotional abuse can be so subtle that even the participants do not "realize" it is taking place. And, where they do realize it, they may not see it clearly as emotional abuse or emotional violence. Emotional abuse wears so many faces and applies so many techniques. (See *Chapter 19.*)

Among numerous other forms of "non-violent" abuse is financial abuse, which can seem so natural to the participants that it remains unlabeled. Yet, just like other forms of abuse, the impacts of financial abuse can last for years, even a lifetime. (See the book with follows this one, *ASK DR. ANGELA #702.*) These and other nonphysical abuses—*hidden violences*—must be recognized and addressed to heal from these and to halt them.

VIOLENCE CAN BE HABIT FORMING

Here is something people avoid talking about: The many dimensions of violence also include the various degrees to which all forms of relationship abuse and violence can become *habitual*—can take on the characteristics of habits, perhaps even addictions.

Yes, violence can become a habit for the person abusing, who is sometimes described as the batterer or the perpetrator, and even sometimes for the person experiencing the violence,

ASK DR. ANGELA® SERIES
ASK DR. ANGELA About Intimate and Other Partner Abuse and Violence

who can be lulled into, forced into, in some way *trapped in a pattern of cyclic abuse.* This *"habit*-uation" all too often grows into a habitual, cyclic, way of life for the couple and the family.

Note that nothing about this cyclic habituation to abuse blames the victim of this abuse. The pressures and dynamics of the intimate partner relationship are powerful and form what are frequently powerful patterns.[2]

VIOLENCE CAN INTERCONNECT WITH OTHER PROBLEMS

Additionally, there are or can be numerous other interrelated, coexisting dimensions of what this book calls IPAVT which can include substance abuse, general anxiety and stress, forms of what is frequently termed PTSD (post-traumatic stress "disorder") and newly understood variations of this PTSD (see the following books, *ASK DR. ANGELA, #702* and *#703*), other psychological conditions, as well as personal histories of abuse prior to the marriage or coupling. These conditions, some of which are described as co-occurring "disorders," can be so intertwined with partner abuse and violence that it is unrealistic to see and to treat these as separate free-standing problems. Especially but not only in the overlap between substance abuse and intimate

---

[2] See the in depth discussion of the emotional and behavioral patterns we form and live by in the book, *NAVIGATING LIFE'S STUFF: DYNAMICS OF PERSONAL CHANGE, BOOK ONE— SENSITIZING TO AND NAVIGATING OUR PROCESSES AND THEIR PATTERNS.* See reading list at the end of this present book.

ASK DR. ANGELA
#701: Emotional and Physical
Abuse in Relationships, Part One

partner violence, there is ample evidence demonstrating significant co-occurrence.

There are those who prefer to separate these conditions, not to link these in any way. This is understandable because they want to prevent abusers "passing the buck" for their own violence, excusing their own violence based on other conditions, such as stress, mental illness, alcohol or drug use, or to having been abused as a child. The position against passing the buck is generally described as an *accountability* point of view which is formed to help persons doing the abusing take responsibility for their actions no matter what has contributed to them.

Indeed, this accountability is a noble approach, and persons abusing should be helped to, even expected to, take this responsibility no matter what contributes to their violence. Still, treating their violence without treating the co-occurring conditions is limiting the power of the work being done with and for persons who wish to stop their abusive behaviors.

QUESTION OF MUTUAL VIOLENCE

And then there is the question of **mutual aggression, mutual violence**. What is and is not **mutual** violence must be examined very carefully, as mutual violence is extremely complex. The old childhood passing of the buck, the "well, you started it" explanation, says very little about who, or which one, is actually at fault—or about whether two people, a few other people, an entire family or community, or no one at all, is at fault. And, the basic meaning of "at fault" is not at all adequately addressed by this "you asked for it" assertion.

ASK DR. ANGELA® SERIES
ASK DR. ANGELA About Intimate and Other Partner Abuse and Violence

The answer to the basic question implied here, the question which asks: *is there typically a <u>dominant</u> aggressor—someone who is clearly the initiator and primary enactor of the physical violence between these two intimate partners—* is frequently debated.

Each case has a different aggressor-victim profile. In fact, law enforcement officers, when arriving at the scene of domestic violence, frequently seek to determine who is the dominant aggressor and take action with regard to this individual. However, when there is not clarity about this, some will say (sometimes perhaps only for convenience' sake) that both members of the couple may be apprehended or at least treated as the primary violent ones, the mutual perpetrators.

Of course, while mutual aggression is quite common, there are countless variations that must be respected. For example, when partners shout or swear at each other, this may be, *may be or may not be,* mutual verbal or emotional abuse. *This in itself is not mutual physical abuse.*

And then, if one of these partners reacts by becoming physically violent against the other (before the other does, or if the other does not), this is *also not considered mutual physical violence.*

Certainly, there are instances where the mutual aggression label is appropriate. However, too often, this label is used by the perpetrator of the violence (**and by those colluding with, and or defending, the perpetrator**) to obscure the reality that the violence is indeed coming from the dominant aggressor who is indeed the true perpetrator. We can hope that

ASK DR. ANGELA
#701: Emotional and Physical Abuse in Relationships, Part One

eventually increased awareness of the actual details and subtleties of intimate partner abuse and violence, and any related terrorizing (IPAV&T) will shed further light, revealing light, on the "games" that can be and are being "played" with this issue of dominant versus mutual aggression.

We can also *hope* that eventually we can be quite definite when there is indeed (or is not) a mutual aggressor situation. But what scientific advance will this take? Even when we do develop the ability to fully calibrate abuses and violences, the dividing line among these will likely remain: the first actual act of actual physical violence, versus everything preceding this.

DANGEROUS RESPONSE DELAY AND EXACERBATION

All this being said, there is a serious need for insight into cases of sudden extreme physical violence. Where a partner who is generally the abus<u>ee</u> rather than the abus<u>er</u> abruptly grows highly, even shockingly violent against the partner, the history of the abuse and violence patterns in these persons' intimate partner relationship must be considered.

While this person who has abruptly become extremely violent will likely be described as the dominant aggressor in this particular instance of violence, there may be a long history of this person being the actual abus<u>ee</u> at the hands of the other partner, frequently being abused and or beaten, and or violated in other ways such as sexual forms of abuse and violence.

ASK DR. ANGELA® SERIES
ASK DR. ANGELA About Intimate and Other Partner Abuse and Violence

Always, the question of how much physical abuse and violence this person has experienced at the hands of the person (who is sometimes indeed the actual abuser) suddenly now being abused must be taken into account.

Has the response to ongoing abuse been delayed? Has the delayed response been exacerbated by the delay itself, delay while the experience of being abused and violated has continued and perhaps even increased in level of danger?

Is there a dangerous backlog of response collected and buried deep within the mind of the person being repeatedly abused over time? Does this backlog perhaps magnify like money in the bank collecting interest?

Are there many instances where the person being abused simply did not respond, or fight back, yet did feel the drive to respond on some very deep, perhaps even subconscious level? Was this drive to respond suppressed, but not eliminated, and left to magnify perhaps? These are questions we must ask. (See *Chapter 5* and *Figure 5.1* for more on this.)

QUESTION OF COLLATERAL VIOLENCE AND ABUSE

A word here about what this book terms: ***collateral violence and abuse***. This is violence that is expressed by one partner against the other—but indirectly and sometimes out of sight (sometimes unseen by the other partner perhaps, and or sometimes unseen by the outside world). *In other words, a*

ASK DR. ANGELA
#701: Emotional and Physical Abuse in Relationships, Part One

person doing the abusing may, instead of abusing the partner directly, abuse someone or something else, in order to threaten or cause fear, pain, expense, or harm of another sort, to the partner. This is abuse.

Although the significance and gravity of what this book describes as collateral violence and abuse deserves far more attention than it gets among professionals and researchers, collateral violence and abuse is quite serious, and can be quite dangerous, damaging, sometimes fatal. While a separate book in this series specifically addressing this matter looks in depth at many forms of, and severe uses of, collateral abuse and violence, here it is important to simply note that this type of indirect partner abuse and violence indeed does exist.

LIST: COLLATERAL IPAVT

This collateral abuse and violence includes but is not limited to threatened or actual, implied or explicit, abuse of and violence against:

Children, for example:

- Where children are purposefully or inadvertently neglected as part of the overall partner abuse scenario.
- Where children are purposefully or inadvertently verbally or emotionally abused as part of the overall abuse scenario.
- Where children of a partner are abused as a way of implicitly abusing the other partner.
- Where children are used as human shields—thrown under the bus so to speak—in effort to ward off abuse of, or detection of abuse by, one or both partners.

ASK DR. ANGELA® SERIES
ASK DR. ANGELA About Intimate and Other Partner Abuse and Violence

- Where children are used in legal processes as trades or implicit trades for assets or other items.
- Where a parent anguishes over the abuse of her or his child by her or his partner and is not able to stop this let alone get help for this often well hidden, *obscured abuse*—while not able to prove this or be believed about this by outsiders or authorities such as the courts.
- Where a child is shown pornography or involved in pornographic filming, and related media by a parent or relative.
- Where a partner is committing child abuse including child sexual abuse.
- Where a partner is committing child sexual abuse and the other partner is explicitly or implicitly threatened with severe retaliation for exposure of this, or for even the possibility of exposure of this.
- Where child sexual abuse committed by one partner is taking place, and the other partner does not know yet experiences the related stresses and problems of the child and family.
- Where a partner threatens to win custody of a child as a form of abuse of the other partner.
- Where a partner threatens to or actually does take or kidnap a child.
- Where a child is forced to observe or know about other "secret" or threatened, or open abuses being performed against family members.

Parents, and or other family members, for example:
- Where all or any of the same, or similarly or equally abusive, behaviors listed above under the category,

ASK DR. ANGELA
#701: Emotional and Physical Abuse in Relationships, Part One

children, take place – against children, parents, or other family members.
- Where abuse of family members and or threats of this abuse are engaged in by a partner.
- Where elder abuse, and or abuse of a person with a disability, and or threats of this abuse are engaged in by a partner.
- Where a partner threatens the safety, well-being, or life of parents or other family members.
- Where parents and other family members are threatened with retaliation for trying to protect the abused partner (or child).

Friends, Neighbors, Community Members, And Co-workers, for example:

- Where all or any of the same, or similarly or equally abusive, behaviors listed above under the category, children, take place.
- Where abuse and or threats of this abuse are engaged in by a partner.
- Where a partner threatens the safety, well-being, or life of friends, neighbors, community members, co-workers, or others.
- Where friends, neighbors, community members, co-workers, and others are threatened with retaliation for trying to protect the abused partner (or child or family member).

Pets, for example:
- Where a partner threatens, steals, or actually directly abuses or kills a pet belonging to, or known by, the partner or family members.

ASK DR. ANGELA® SERIES
ASK DR. ANGELA About Intimate and Other Partner Abuse and Violence

Property, for example:

- Where a partner threatens or actually engages in the stealing, hiding, re-labeling, withholding, devaluing, damaging, or destroying of property and assets belonging to or shared by the other partner or family members, friends, and or others around the relationship.

Earning power, etc., for example:

- Where a partner engages in harm to the other partner's career, work-life, etc. via messaging, information withholding or distorting, slanderous or similar reputation affecting activities, paycheck or money withholding—as well as interference with:

  partner's ability to acquire a job, keep a job, perform on the job, look good at work, be at work on time, to utilize the paycheck earned, and so on (*with children, parents, and or others being abused in the same way as part of this scenario*).

COLLATERAL TERROR

The above is a list of just some of the many forms of collateral abuse and violence that may be present in IPAV&T situations. In reading this book, keep in mind that all too often actual, front and center, IPAV&T may be taking place alongside harder to see "background" collateral abuses, violences, and terrorizations. These may be subtle and even

ASK DR. ANGELA
#701: Emotional and Physical Abuse in Relationships, Part One

hidden abuses, however these are powerful and must be addressed for all involved.

Ultimately, most if not all forms of collateral abuse and violence can be and likely are terrorization of the partner and of all others involved.

TERRORIZATION AS ABUSE

Terrorization is the inflicting of fear of harm and or of actual harm, simply to inflict this fear and or actual harm, and or to *control, retaliate against, persuade, motivate, stifle, or suppress* someone via inflicting fear and or actual harm. Using and abusing children, family members, others, pets, incomes, and so on to control a partner is a common form of relatively indirect terrorization. That this is "indirect" terrorization is that this is done not directly to the abusee but to others around the abusee or to the abusee's property.

This indirect terrorization frequently has as intense and painful an impact as does direct terrorization. For example, when the abuser abuses the partner by abusing the child, this is as great if not greater a terrorization than is the direct beating or molesting or raping of that abusee.

Other forms of terrorization of a partner are somewhat more direct and are equally frightening and painful and therefore terror invoking. The fields addressing intimate partner violence must add this form of abuse to the lexicon and description of this violence and abuse: terror, both direct and indirect forms of terror.

ASK DR. ANGELA® SERIES
ASK DR. ANGELA About Intimate and Other Partner Abuse and Violence

Note that another form of this terror is the long term outcome of intimate partner violence and abuse. As noted elsewhere in this book, and other books in this series, studies are indicating that there are significant long term health impacts found in especially women who have experienced earlier IPV and IPAV. While many of the effects, much of the harm and damage generated by IPV and IPAV reveals itself as it is being inflicted, much of the harm and damage surfaces far later. This is an unseen aspect of the abuse and violence, for many a later surfacing condition, injury, even terror.

ASK DR. ANGELA
#701: Emotional and Physical
Abuse in Relationships, Part One

Chapter 4
Last Time Story

In the midst of a loud verbal argument, he yelled, "You stupid idiot, you know I'm right!" He raised his arm as if he would hit her if she did not agree.

She jumped back and yelled, "Don't you dare hit me, you look so stupid doing that!"

In that moment, as she was saying this, he leapt forward, right at her, swinging his arm as he did, this time hitting her in the face, tearing the skin to the side of her head near the eye, and leaving a red mark which would later become a black eye.

Stunned and flinching in pain, she fell to her knees, covering her eye, saying, "Stop! That's the last time you'll ever hit me!"

He grumbled back, "Oh yeah, who's going to stop me?"

"I'll call the police."

"No, you won't. You bitch, get up and go wash your face, it's bleeding all over the carpet. And then, clean this mess up. Or I'll kick you so hard you won't ever be the same."

"This is your fault, you do it," she said. But she finally cleaned it up anyway. She felt this was the safer option.

ASK DR. ANGELA® SERIES
ASK DR. ANGELA About Intimate and Other Partner
Abuse and Violence

ASK DR. ANGELA
#701: Emotional and Physical
Abuse in Relationships, Part One

Chapter 5
All About Intentions

What is overlooked in many instances, perhaps because it is difficult to determine (or sometimes because one or all of the involved parties prefer not to make it clear), is *intent*. Intent matters very much, yet it is largely misunderstood. Additionally, both actual and manufactured confusion—regarding the difference between conscious intent and unconscious intent—exists among onlookers and well as among those directly involved in the relationship violence.

INTENT IS DIFFICULT TO DETERMINE AND OFTEN DISGUISED

How frequently we hear it said, "I did not mean to hurt you," and "it isn't my fault because I did it on impulse," and "you made me do it," and "I had no intention of knocking your tooth out when I raised my hand at you and hit you, that was an accident."

This and other passing off of responsibility for causing harm and injury is loaded with tricky, elusive, often devious deception—deception of others as well as *self deception*. Deception is used like a weapon although the true nature of the deception is typically hidden from awareness.

ASK DR. ANGELA® SERIES
ASK DR. ANGELA About Intimate and Other Partner Abuse and Violence

The utility of deception to the person deceiving is profound. Lies can be camouflaged in its mazes. A sea of confusion can be pulled in, drowning both the abus<u>er</u> and the abus<u>ee</u> in the lies. Basically, deception confuses everyone around abuse.

Persons abusing and then choosing to deceive about their abusing sometimes invest in their lies, in their denial of the abuse they have perpetrated. They suggest they are so very convinced of their own innocence.

In so doing, they frequently go so far as to reconstruct —even reconstitute— themselves as the victims (see the following books, #702 and #703, for more on this). Examples of this sort of **illusion-constructing around abuse** can also be found in families, communities, and even in the courts.

The tables can be turned, sometimes in a split second, with the abus<u>ee</u> suddenly and convincingly recast as the abus<u>er</u>, and vice versa. This is where persons around persons who abuse (such as spouses, partners, family members, friends, colleagues, therapists, medical doctors, attorneys, courts) may be unwittingly (largely unwittingly) pulled into <u>colluding with abusers</u> who make this sort of choice—to turn the tables against the true victim, to do this to deny, strike down, abuse charges.

These persons who abuse may do everything to deny that they abuse, be very skilled at doing this, and succeed in pulling others into believing and even supporting their lies. The credibility of the person being abused is then called into question, the integrity of the person who originally reported the abuse is attacked, a tactic frequently seen in court room strategies.

ASK DR. ANGELA
#701: Emotional and Physical Abuse in Relationships, Part One

Truth becomes a game or a strategy rather than a reality. A crafty abuser can actually extend the abuse of the partner right into the courtroom, at times even managing to engage some attorneys and judges as colluders.

Deception itself is deceiving and unfortunately can be a useful tool.

There are areas that are so very difficult to unravel that they are flat out avoided for convenience and simplicity's sake as well as for reasons involving *fear of truth*. Even avoidance or muddling of truth for the sake of simplicity is all too common. Questions such as these can be both ignored and played out by all involved:

Where is the line between intent and mistake?

Who defines this line, and who should be defining this line?

What should we require of those we expect to define this line?

When does the subconscious mind accommodate its conscious lies by calling certain actions only mistakes, not intentional abuse?

When does the mind fool itself about the use of violence when angry?

How does the abuser find support for the blurring of the truth?

Isn't the abuser's purposeful blurring of the truth itself a form of abuse?

ASK DR. ANGELA® SERIES
ASK DR. ANGELA About Intimate and Other Partner Abuse and Violence

LINES BETWEEN INTENT AND IMPULSE

These are important but difficult questions that require honest answers (where answers are possible). Yet, when it comes to violence, the lines between intent and impulse, and also between intent and mistake, are blurry, and there is significant overlap (see *Figure 5.2*).

Even in courts of law, these things are not exceedingly clear. Consider the legal concept, *mens rea*, which refers to the mental state when committing a crime. A great deal of debate takes place in courts of law regarding the state of mind a person who committed a crime was in when committing it. Four basic mental states are considered in asking—was this crime committed: intentionally, knowingly, recklessly, or negligently.

At first glance, answers to this question may seem obvious. After all, the person either meant to do it or did not. The assumption is that: it is possible to determine whether or not the person who committed the crime knew what he or she was doing and meant to do it. Again, was the crime committed: intentionally, knowingly, recklessly, or negligently. And will the perpetrator of the abuse be honest here?

Where, even in a court of law, intent is heavily debated, the court of the mind is murkier than the letter of judicial law would like it to be. From a psychological standpoint, the overlap among and between these areas of intent can tend to blur the distinctions so much that they cannot be successfully separated.

ASK DR. ANGELA
#701: Emotional and Physical Abuse in Relationships, Part One

We might like to say: Of course, human beings have developed to a point where it should be relatively easy to make a distinction between willful action and mistake. We know the difference, right? We must ask ourselves questions like this.

How many times have we stepped on someone else's toe by mistake? This is neither impulse violence nor premeditated violence—this is almost always simply a mistake or clumsy error. We know this. (We still care about the toe, still would like to provide assistance with the pain.)

What about other injurious acts? What can we take responsibility for and what can we realistically deny responsibility for? Could it be that we should even accept responsibility for our mistakes? (Yes?)

These are complex questions further made blurry by the role of the conscious, subconscious, and unconscious mind in influencing and directing actions people take. On the one hand, there is a range of intent, say intent to commit violence, which is rather obvious, running something like this:

**accidental violence→impulse violence→
→purposeful violence→planned violence**

And, on the other hand, there is a range of degree of consciousness in action such as this:

**unintentional→subconscious intent→
→conscious intent→planned conscious intent**

We could draw these as overlapping fields (as in *Figure 5.2*) or we could graph these two ranges against each other and find actions scattered all over this graph (as in *Figure 5.3*).

VIOLENCE AS A DEFENSIVE RESPONSE

Typically, but not always, even if both resort to physical violence, one of the partners initiates it (or escalates first to actual physical and strikes first). Explanations for why this violence was initiated first or at all vary and can differ from each of the partners and from witnesses (if any). Quite often, impulse is the explanation, whether or not this is what is said explains the violence. Impulse warrants close attention here as sometimes impulse violence is definitely assault and other times impulse violence is something else.

Immediate impulse driven action which may include violence is one of the natural responses to actual and perceived as being actual danger. This response is most frequently described in terms of the "fight or flight" reflex. Fight or flight is an instinctive response to a situation which requires immediate action—for actual or presumed survival reasons.

Fight or flight says: when escaping or simply getting out of a dangerous predicament is not perceived as an option, then fighting back is another response which is available. An animal trapped in a corner, seeing no way to escape a predator, will likely try to fight back or perhaps even attack the predator.

ASK DR. ANGELA
#701: Emotional and Physical
Abuse in Relationships, Part One

What other option is there? Perhaps rolling over and playing dead? (Playing dead can be called the "freeze" response, and is almost as common as fight or flight. Freezing is an attempt to hide, blend in, be undetected or not seen, camouflage for safety.) Instinct of course does not require that the animal stop to think the options through.

This ancient fight or flight (or freeze) reflex snaps into place on the spot by means of a **biochemical automatic rapid response system** we carry with us at all times. Biology speaks. (However, this biological rapid response system does not always function appropriately or at all for that matter. See the subsection below on **suppressed response** for more on this matter.)

However consistently well it functions, the fight or flight reflex can be and sometimes is an ingredient in intimate partner violence. For example, during a heated argument, one of the partners may read danger with no escape in the situation, whether or not this no escape is truly there, and allow him or herself to snap (or simply be unable to stop him or herself from snapping) into immediate violent action.

Of course, quite frequently, one of the partners does not "initiate" the violence yet the other one does while using something---something about the other partner's appearance, tone, gesture, or mood, to excuse (or explain, or allow) responding with violence.

However, this using of something to excuse something else is not always purposeful or conscious during the violent event. All too often, excusing the violence takes place after the event, sometimes even in the court room. Of course, there are also many cases where the perpetrator of the violence does excuse the violence even as it is being perpetrated in a "you asked for it" or "what choice do I have here" sort of assertion.

Now, look a little more closely at the arguing couple. The two of them are arguing, growing louder and angrier by the minute, and gesturing more and more adamantly as they proceed. Suddenly, one gesture one of them makes is seen (or used) by the other as escalation. In this moment, a threat is picked up (or a threat is said to be taking place), and physical danger seems (or is said to be) imminent.

A split second into seeing or sensing this (or pretending to sense this), sometimes without thinking about it at all, reflex may kick in. This person may suddenly perceive (or choose to perceive) this gesturing as threatening and meaning:

Danger!
Now!

Reacting to seeming (or what is claimed to be) immediate physical danger, even perhaps as this danger is manifesting into a real attack, perhaps as it is not, this person swings first.

Now it IS physical.

**Yet now the
first strike is perhaps ambiguous.**

ASK DR. ANGELA
#701: Emotional and Physical
Abuse in Relationships, Part One

NUANCES OF
SUPPRESSED FIGHT OR FLIGHT RESPONSE

As noted in the *Chapter 3* (subsection titled, *Dangerous Response Delay and Exacerbation*), we must consider a largely unaddressed yet quite critical condition in which relationship violence can occur. Let's note also here the discussion immediately above regarding the fight or flight reflex. Now consider the possibility that there may be instances or cases where this reflex does not fully or effectively function in a timely manner—or does not function at all.

Various other mechanisms can intercede or even block this precious fight or flight reflex. Consider the chart in Figure 4.1., offering examples of where there appears no fight or flight response to potential or actual danger or harm. In this chart, either the flight function is confused or overridden, or the fight function is. These particular victims of this violence either:

- **do not realize they are in danger, or**
- **do not see that getting away is NEEDED, or**
- **do not feel it is WISE to get away from this danger, or**
- **do not feel SAFE trying to get away from this danger, or**
- **do not feel that getting away from this danger is POSSIBLE.**

ASK DR. ANGELA® SERIES
ASK DR. ANGELA About Intimate and Other Partner Abuse and Violence

For a range of reasons, the ability to take flight, to get away from potential or actual danger is thwarted or stalled or blocked by INability to see the NEED to get away, or to see that getting away is WISE, SAFE, and or POSSIBLE. Persons who have been abused in extreme ways, and or in psychologically repressing or distorting ways, may experience, be pressed to accept, this abuse in these ways.

However, the abuse is indeed being experienced whether or not it is consciously acknowledged. After a while, in ongoing abuse situations, where the victim of this abuse represses or does not tap into the fight or flight reflex, *deep neural memories* of experiencing this abuse and violence can be registered or stored. It may be never or quite a while later when suddenly, unexpectedly, not necessarily logically, the person being abused releases a *mountain of repressed fight or flight responses.* Now, to speak in common terms, this long abused person may suddenly "lose it" and may sometimes become quite violent with self or others.

To outsiders who have no idea what the mind of this abused person has stockpiled as it has found no previous outlet, this abrupt and often wild behavior is shocking and appalling. Suddenly, the long time and severely abused person appears to outsiders to be the abus<u>er</u>. *Now the abus<u>ee</u>'s mountain of stockpiled rage and self defense response is seemingly being (to onlookers) ignited for no fair reason.*

Now the person being abused may grow abruptly, and perhaps virtually, uncontrollably emotionally or even physically violent.

ASK DR. ANGELA
#701: Emotional and Physical Abuse in Relationships, Part One

Now this abusEE may be releasing a great deal of *pent up impulse response*, all that suppressed and or blocked fight or flight—that backlog of unexpressed yet present somewhere response.

In the particular instance where such an abusee suddenly and fiercely abuses, the abusee is suddenly committing first strike in so far as onlookers may discern. Yet for the abusEE, the forced roller coaster ride began long before this moment.

This is the moment where what may surface is the abusEE's long withheld response to the other partner's, the abusER's, first strikes....

VIOLENCE IS LIKE AN ONION

But let's go back to any so-called "typical fighting couple." There they go again. On and on. And on. OK. Stop. Pause the tape. Freeze. No one move. What really happened here?

Chances are each of these persons will report a somewhat different sequence of events, a somewhat different sequence of escalation, and a different primary aggressor. Will one of them be lying?

Was the dominant aggressor the one who shifted to a highly threatening gesture which actually could have become a hit, or could have become perceived (or chosen to be perceived) as a coming hit? Or was the one who responded reflexively by hitting first the dominant aggressor?

ASK DR. ANGELA® SERIES
ASK DR. ANGELA About Intimate and Other Partner Abuse and Violence

Does their history of first strikes and previous violence matter here? **Yes, as this clarifies the pattern.** *Seeing the pattern preceding an event helps to clarify it. Most if not all relationship events take place within relationship patterns.*

Too frequently, the person abusing, beating the abusee violently even viciously, will say "well, you shouted," or "well, you stood in my way," or "you provoked this on purpose, you knew how I would have to respond," or "I'm a big animal so next time don't provoke me. If you provoke me and get hurt, it's your fault."

Perhaps the answer here in this sort of situation lies not in the question of dominance per se, but in the question of type of aggression. *At what point did the aggression become physical?* At the time of the first hit? Or of the first seemingly threatening physical gesture? Is there a point where the gestures or the body language of one or both became truly physically threatening? *(Or, is there a moment when one of the partners* ***pretends*** *that the other partner is threatening?)* Again, it does help to ask:

Is there a history here, one of threatened and actual violence and first strikes, a pattern which would explain more?

And what about situations where one partner is more physically capable than the other? Does the partner who can dominate simply by being physically stronger become the actual or implied dominant aggressor almost naturally amidst conflict or leading up to conflict?

ASK DR. ANGELA
#701: Emotional and Physical Abuse in Relationships, Part One

How does this play out when both partners are waving hands and shouting at each other while both know that one is physically more dangerous, or at least stronger and therefore dominant? Clearly, physical dominance brings with it a natural albeit largely implied physical power.

But stop. Roll the tape back again.

Can we get into the minds of members of this relationship to see precisely where the violence actually originated? How fine should our unit of analysis be? How much detail do we want to see? How far back, and back to what, do we go?

Where is the truth hiding? If we continue peeling the layers back, we find more layers. Intimate partner violence is so very layered; its true origins may truly elude us. This complexity and layering make it easy for lies about intent to be believed!

This mix of complexity and layering make it easy for a dominant aggressor to blame the person being abused for the aggression. What a place to hide truth—in the maze of complexity and layering.

VIOLENCE AND IMPLIED VIOLENCE FOR DOMINANCE

Now, let's come at this another way. Let's consider the circumstance where an individual feels—or senses—that his or her **control over and power within** the relationship is being threatened. Assume for a moment that this circumstance involves no threatening gestures or suggestions that actual physical violence is in the wings. *Just see this as a perceived*

ASK DR. ANGELA® SERIES
ASK DR. ANGELA About Intimate and Other Partner Abuse and Violence

threat to one's dominance—where the ego, or the control over the relationship (or the power one has within the relationship) —is seen as being challenged, eroded, curtailed.

Sometimes challenges are felt by simple shifts away from a partner's usual or traditional behavior. In a long term (or even a short term where patterns are already instilled) relationship, sometimes one partner changes. This sometimes upsets the *unspoken founding contract* that apparently "said" that this partner would never change (or change much). Even when this change is personal growth or success, this may be felt to be a breaking of the contract, of the foundation of the relationship. This may, in some cases, even be seen–or not seen consciously but experienced on some level—*as betrayal.*

Let's say a relationship began with one of the partners having more say in decisions. This may have been because one partner was older or had more experience, or made more money. Or it could have been that one partner was a stronger or more confident personality in some way. Or other possibilities exist, such as one partner was raised to feel entitled to dominance – and the other partner was raised not to feel this way.

There are countless reasons for various **power distribution arrangements** *in relationships, many of these logical, even reasonable. However, there are times when* <u>**the power distribution is abused**</u>.

Let's roll the tape back again. See that the two of them are still arguing, growing louder and angrier by the minute, and gesturing more and more adamantly as they proceed.

ASK DR. ANGELA
#701: Emotional and Physical
Abuse in Relationships, Part One

Suddenly, one comment one of them makes is seen (or used) by the other as escalation. In this moment, a threat is picked up, OR A THREAT IS INVENTED AS AN EXCUSE, and some kind of danger seems (or is said to be) imminent. This situation can indeed bring out a fight response. However, quite often something else is being threatened, something other than physical safety.

The danger is now one which threatens to upset the balance of power, or the desired balance of power, in the relationship. Something is said or done that appears to challenge the dominant person's view of his or her right to this dominance and his or her security that this dominance will continue. Something triggers in this person a show of force.

So, is this show of force unintentional, impulsive, or purposeful? Should we call this **unintentional** violence? If this is violence as a defensive response, is this violence defending something which should be defended at all, let alone violently?

Now, there are times when violence (or threatened violence) is consciously—intentionally—resorted to, or applied, to exert, maintain, or demonstrate dominance in a given situation or conflict. Persons exerting violence to maintain power and control over a situation (and or over a person) find no other way to do so. Or they find violence the most certain way to do so.

After all, a vote or a clear conversation about who wants what may not result in what the dominant partner wants. The dominant partner frequently wants to hold onto dominance.

ASK DR. ANGELA® SERIES
ASK DR. ANGELA About Intimate and Other Partner Abuse and Violence

Still, even perpetrators of this sort of violence tend to say that their violence—if they admit to it at all—is impulsive, out of their control. They may go ahead and label this as an impulsive and defensive response. There are even times when comments such as this are made: "Don't blame me, I couldn't help it."

WHEN DEFENDING PRESUMED POWER

Even when the violence is not planned in advance, when it is impulse violence, the use of violence to maintain or gain dominance is rarely entirely impulsive. This is because violence is both physical and nonphysical; violence exists along a continuum (as noted earlier).

This continuum includes many nonphysical violences that are frequently substitutes for, and even precursors of, physical violence. Many elements of violence and abuse are subtle, confusing, sometimes <u>purposefully hidden</u> for the various reasons discussed in this and the following books. These behaviors must be watched by members of the relationship so as to avoid the effects of violence and abuse growing ever more serious.

There is a spoken and also oft unspoken assumption (or excuse) that the use of violence has a so called "reason." This reason is either *self protection*—or an incorrectly assumed "rightful" *control over and dominance of another person*—or both when what is being protected is the abuser's self-defined:

**entitlement to
power and control, dominance
over the partner.**

ASK DR. ANGELA
#701: Emotional and Physical Abuse in Relationships, Part One

Indeed, this is frequently the case. There is usually some form of power (or perceived power) to be acquired (or protected, or regained) by threatening or actually using violence.

THE NEED FOR POWER

This "need" for power in a relationship warrants a whole discussion of its own. In this book (*#701*) and the books which follow (*#702, #703, and #704*), this matter will be further addressed as the subtle complexities of intimate partner violence, abuse, and terror are further examined.

Basically, the desire of one partner—or sometimes but less often of both partners—for one-sided power and dominance can drive violence in troubled relationships. Some will even claim that actual efforts to gain dominance—***and or to protect dominance already gained***—are driven by instinct, even when the *power and control mentality* is registering in the conscious mind.

Some will claim that they have a right to the power they seek to acquire via the application of force. This "right" as it is sometimes called is explained in various ways reflecting interpretations of and differences in upbringing, tradition, belief system, faith leader teachings, cultural views of women and men and gender roles, law and policy, and more.

TWO FACES OF VIOLENCE

Intent here can be seen both ways: the abuser's intent and the abusee's intent. Abus**ee**? Does this suggest that the victim intends in any way to be victimized? No. ***We do not want to***

ASK DR. ANGELA® SERIES
ASK DR. ANGELA About Intimate and Other Partner Abuse and Violence

blame victims of violence for experiencing the violence. This sort of unfair, unjust, and cruel blame is too frequently heard about rape (as per the "she asked for it" excuse), and also about other forms of *boundary violation (VIO-lation)*. Being careful not to blame the victim here, we still do want to understand the dances couples do around their power conflicts, stresses, and differing views. And we want to know more about the way some couples can do their dances without getting hurt or hurting, while others do eventually hurt, or damage, or maim, and or sometimes even kill.

And this damaging, maiming, and killing can indeed be either physical or nonphysical—can be varying aspects and forms of damage, injury, and death. This damaging can truly affect, in both the short and the long term, health, body, mind, and spirit, whether or not the physical body explicitly shows this.

In this sense, given that the nonphysical aspects of violence and abuse tend to be overlooked and denied, the *invisible* injuries (and costs of those injuries) relationship abuse and violence can bring are perhaps the most insidious and difficult to address.

An entire treatise could be written (as a later book in this series does write) regarding the *invisible—unseen, sometimes denied, other times not recognized by any party*—effects and injuries inflicted or generated by relationship abuse and violence. Here, this book (and the books that follow, #702, #703) will return several times to this matter, always with the following proviso or caveat: Many abuses and violences immediately or eventually result in one or both of these:

ASK DR. ANGELA
#701: Emotional and Physical Abuse in Relationships, Part One

- obvious and distinct physical and emotional effects, with some of these effects being injuries; and
- subtle and oft hidden effects, with some of these effects being physical and emotional injuries surfacing in present time or far later.

INTENTS OF PARTNER ABUSE AND VIOLENCE

We who have been, are, or will be, members of an intimate partner (IP) relationship do well to ask ourselves some of these challenging questions, questions we may tend to avoid. Among these questions is another tough one: what elements of a sort of (what the books in this series call) emotional sado-masochism (with or without parallel emotional masochism)—or of some form of agreement to allow one member of the couple to intentionally cause hurt (and the other to receive it)—are present or potentially present in the relationship being considered? These are difficult questions, even troubling. (See also the following books in this series, *#702, #703, and #704.*)

How can anyone even imagine that the victim of abuse is somehow complicit in inflicting the partner's abuse upon her or himself? Who would intend to do such a thing to her or himself? Who?

QUESTIONS TO ASK ABOUT INTENT

Clearly, intention is a touchy topic here. We must ask:

ASK DR. ANGELA® SERIES
ASK DR. ANGELA About Intimate and Other Partner Abuse and Violence

- Who intends to even sometimes, maybe only once in a while, hurt someone else?
- Who intends to allow someone else to hurt her or himself?
- Who intends to actually hurt her or himself let alone anyone else? Who?
- And who could take pleasure in, or feel rewarded in some way by, hurting another?
- And who could take pleasure in, or feel rewarded in some way by, hurting her or himself? Who?
- And who may find safety in consciously choosing to experience more of a known abuse rather than risk experiencing an unknown and potentially far more dangerous abuse?

Daring to ask might give us answers that would help identify dangers before they surface, emerging streams of inclinations, tendencies, vulnerabilities, and dangers.

INVESTMENT IN PARTNER VIOLENCE

Another related and touchy, even unasked, question is this: Is there the possibility that one or both members of the couple may, unknowingly or even consciously, become addicted to a pattern of emotional sadomasochism, or to the adrenalin rush this behavior may invite, or to the emotional/sexual pleasure it may bring on during the acts it involves or after these acts (such as during the makeup sex). We must dare to seek the truths we tend to deny about troubled relationships.

Now we must ask: *What **emotional investment**, no matter how potentially self destructive, do one or both members of the couple*

ASK DR. ANGELA
#701: Emotional and Physical Abuse in Relationships, Part One

(either knowingly or unknowingly) have in the **behavioral patterning of the troubled relationship?** Is the pattern the couple is caught in one that carries hidden rewards such as flowers, hugs, gifts, and sex during make-ups?[3]

REQUIRES A DEEP HONEST LOOK

Key to preventing and or healing abusive relationships is a deep, honest, and unique understanding of the dynamics, not just of abusive relationships, and of habitually abusive relationships, but also of all intimate partner relationships. What elements — or at least traces — of all the above and more are found in both healthy and troubled relationships? (Many relationships do function well and keep these traces at bay.)

What spoken and unspoken contracts addressing these elements are made? What contracts should be made? What contracts are broken? What contracts break themselves? And what contracts are only imagined in the first place? How clear can we be on all this?

And, what about trust — is trust relevant here? How important is trust in successful relationships? Does trust slip into the background, and even dissolve away, in hurting relationships?

Could it be that in some instances troubled partners reach a point where they trust each other, yes, but trust each other to play out the troubled roles they have defined for each other — even when these

---

[3] See the book where this patterning and its effects are discussed in greater depth: *NAVIGATING LIFE'S STUFF: DYNAMICS OF PERSONAL CHANGE, BOOK ONE.*

roles are sad, painful, and dangerous? These are instances of investment in the troubled pattern.

Let's explore these and other questions in the following chapters of this book (*#701*), and then the following books in this series (*#702, #703, and #704*) where these roles and some of their troubled interactions are slowed to see these.

ASK DR. ANGELA
#701: Emotional and Physical Abuse in Relationships, Part One

THERE IS DEFINITE POTENTIAL OR ACTUAL PHYSICAL DANGER, HARM, YET....	FLIGHT does not appear to be NEEDED	FLIGHT does not appear to be WISE	FLIGHT does not appear to be SAFE	FLIGHT does not appear to be POSSIBLE
FIGHT does not appear to be NEEDED	Fight does not appear to be NEEDED, while flight does not appear NEEDED—are these two perceptions interfering with each other?	Fight does not appear to be NEEDED, while flight does not appear WISE—are these two perceptions interfering with each other?	Fight does not appear to be NEEDED, while flight does not appear SAFE—are these two perceptions interfering with each other?	Fight does not appear to be NEEDED, while flight does not appear POSSIBLE—are these two perceptions interfering with each other?
FIGHT does not appear to be WISE	Fight does not appear to be WISE, while flight does not appear NEEDED—are these two perceptions interfering with each other?	Fight does not appear to be WISE, while flight does not appear WISE—are these two perceptions interfering with each other?	Fight does not appear to be WISE, while flight does not appear SAFE—are these two perceptions interfering with each other?	Fight does not appear to be WISE, while flight does not appear POSSIBLE—are these two perceptions interfering with each other?
FIGHT does not appear to be SAFE	Fight does not appear to be SAFE, while flight does not appear NEEDED—are these two perceptions interfering with each other?	Fight does not appear to be SAFE, while flight does not appear WISE—are these two perceptions interfering with each other?	Fight does not appear to be SAFE, while flight does not appear SAFE—are these two perceptions interfering with each other?	Fight does not appear to be SAFE, while flight does not appear POSSIBLE—are these two perceptions interfering with each other?
FIGHT does not appear to be POSSIBLE	Fight does not appear to be POSSIBLE, while flight does not appear NEEDED—are these two perceptions interfering with each other?	Fight does not appear to be POSSIBLE, while flight does not appear WISE—are these two perceptions interfering with each other?	Fight does not appear to be POSSIBLE, while flight does not appear SAFE—are these two perceptions interfering with each other?	Fight does not appear to be POSSIBLE, while flight does not appear POSSIBLE—are these two perceptions interfering with each other?

Figure 5.1. Examples of possibly suppressed fight or flight response.

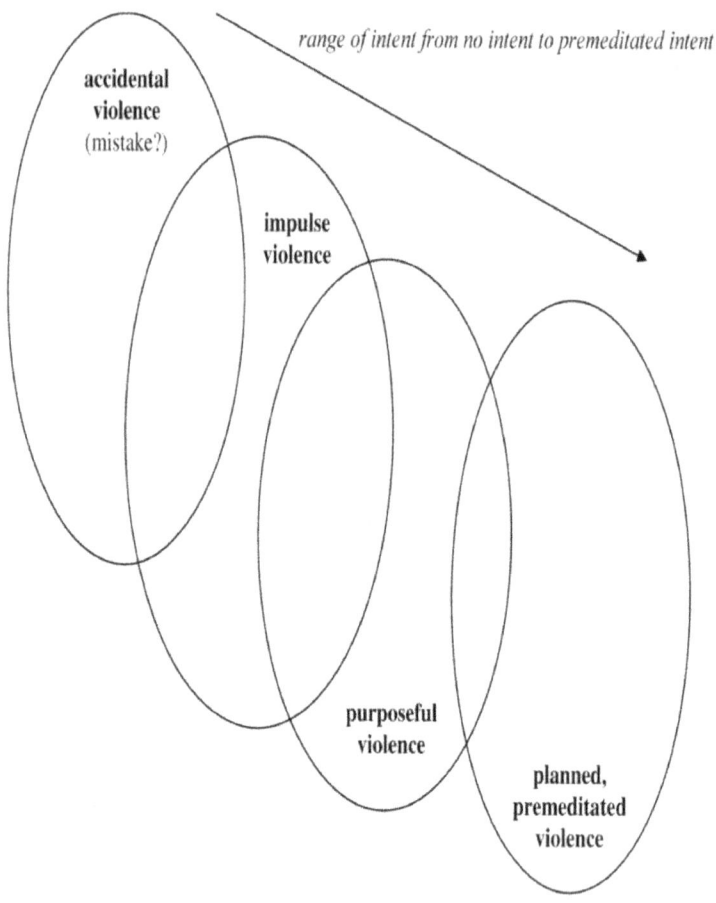

Figure 5.2. Blurry spectrum of partner violence intent.

ASK DR. ANGELA
#701: Emotional and Physical Abuse in Relationships, Part One

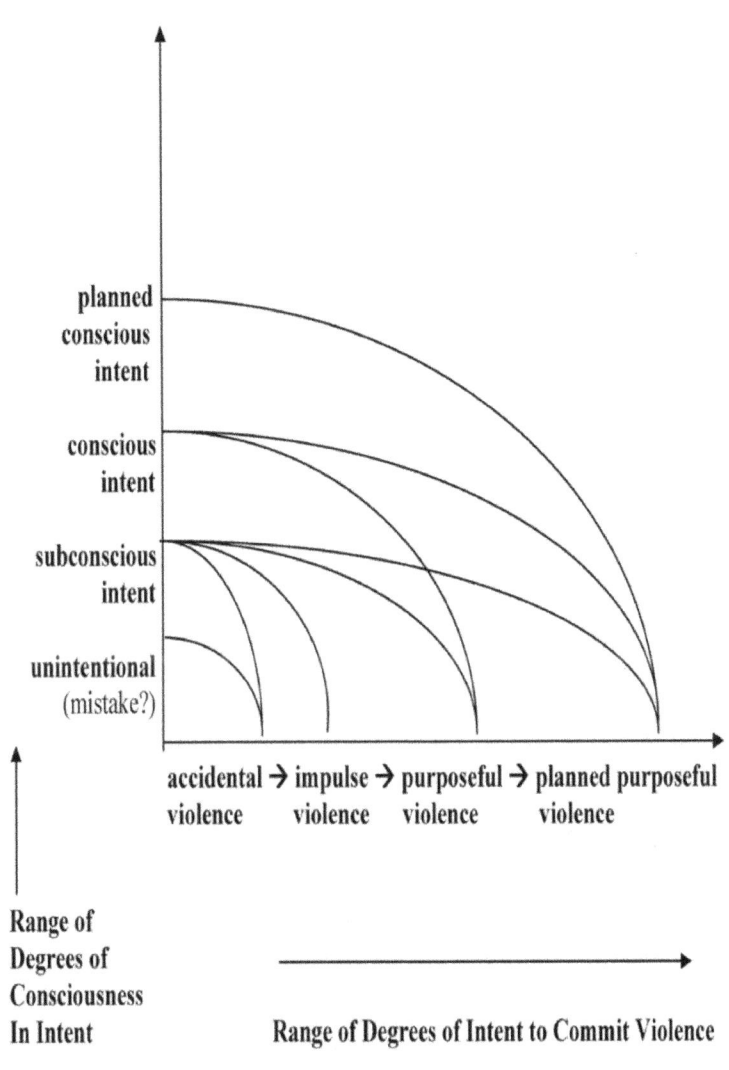

Figure 5.3. Graph of two ranges of intent.

ASK DR. ANGELA® SERIES
ASK DR. ANGELA About Intimate and Other Partner Abuse and Violence

ASK DR. ANGELA
#701: Emotional and Physical
Abuse in Relationships, Part One

Chapter 6
What About Consent

Welcome to the wilderness of human behavior. Here, we can find great wonderment and joy.

Yet here, in some, not many but some, relationships, we may find perils and monsters lurking in the shadows: misunderstandings, misinterpretations, anxieties and fears, risks and dangers. And yet, we may say, "yes, I'm staying."

CONSENT IS MISUNDERSTOOD

If getting at intent is challenging, add in the matter of consent and find a wilderness of human behavior to wade through. When a person who abuses claims not to mean it, or that the person being abused "wants it," what on Earth can this mean? Frequently, this means simply that the person abusing wants to place blame on someone else for the abusive behavior. Sometimes this means that the person doing the abusing did not recognize the abuse as abuse as the other party *seemed to be* participating in the situation, the game, the interaction, with full consent. Seemed to be. Seemed?

All too often, persons being abused who attempt to bring their cases to court are told, "You stayed, so you were consenting," and "You clearly are smart enough to leave if you were being abused, so clearly you were not being abused. THEREFORE YOUR CLAIMS ARE FALSE."

ASK DR. ANGELA® SERIES
ASK DR. ANGELA About Intimate and Other Partner Abuse and Violence

ENABLING THE ABUSE OF CONSENT

In love, sex, and related human behaviors, consent is one of the most misunderstood elements of interactions. Consent is generally defined as agreeing voluntarily, giving permission. Let's stop right here. What a loaded definition this is!

First take each word separately: "agreeing," "voluntarily," "giving," and "permission."

Agreeing can take many forms, and agreements can be clear and or vague (and or in reality nonexistent). We have all heard the teaching offered to teenagers facing sexual activity early in their lives: "no means no." Yet how often "no" is misunderstood for yes, by both the person being told "no" and yes, sometimes even by the person saying "no." Both parties must understand that no means no and that is that.

What does this messy use of the word "no" do to the act of agreeing? And what does this do to the act of agreeing *voluntarily*? There is nothing voluntary about being forced to do something and this is, of course, simple to understand. *Yet, there are degrees of force, and sources of force.*

For example, someone forcing someone else to engage in sex against her or his will is committing rape. *This is crossing boundaries without permission. This is indeed boundary crossing, however quite frequently this is not viewed this way.* Yet, what about social or emotional pressure to do something, including engage in sex, against one's will? Is this force, and if so, is this rape? Again, the law may rightly have distinct categories for these behaviors, and yet these may be far more

ASK DR. ANGELA
#701: Emotional and Physical Abuse in Relationships, Part One

complex than law may allow. There is no limit to the shades of agreeing voluntarily, and to the misuse of these shades when blaming the victim.

The infinite shades and nuances of consent and non-consent are always at work in human interactions, especially in intimate partner, significant other, dating, and similar relationships.

Now, add in the confusion about "giving permission." "Giving" itself is often misunderstood. How many times do we hear a dialog like this? "Hey, that's mine!" "No, it isn't, you gave it to me." How many times is the act of giving entirely misunderstood by both the receiving party and the giving party?

And what is this thing we call *permission*? Having permission is generally defined as being allowed to do something, having authorization to do it. This suggests (assumes) that the person giving permission is able enough and free enough to consciously allow a behavior, and then freely authorizes this behavior. This also suggests (assumes) that the person consenting is informed enough, mature enough, healthy enough, and *safe enough*, to freely give conscious consent.

CONSENT AND INTENT

Now that we have this matter of consent on the table, let's serve it up with the intent discussed in the previous chapter. How might all this play out in an abusive situation? Does the person being abused give some form of consent—even if it is unspoken consent—to the abuse? Or is this simply a bizarre and cruel distortion of what is taking or has taken place, what is claimed by some persons who are abusing—or who are defending abusers?

Does and could the person abusing, abuse with intent to respond to unspoken yet *assumed consent*? This sounds odd, wrong, and yet this interpretation of behavior—somehow thinking (or at least saying) that consent has been given by the other person, the partner—might be sometimes taken, at least subconsciously (and or consciously yet dishonestly), as permission to abuse.

Yet, "permission to abuse me" is rarely given in words if given at all. The notion that there is such a thing as consensual violence—where one person beats another with that another's permission—is questionable. How often do we hear people directly tell their abusers "please beat me up," or "please hurt me for me." (Later chapters in this book, #701, and the following books, #702 and #703, discuss less common yet also important to consider emotionally sadomasochistic relationships.)

PRETENDED CONFUSION

We must look for ways we can get past the confusion in relationships where abuses and violences are taking place. We must also look for ways we can get around the *pretended confusion* in some of these relationships. *Too often, a person being abused is told by a person doing the abusing that the abuse was agreed to therefore it was not abuse. Too often, the person being abused succumbs to the view of the abuser and at least subtly agrees (possibly out of fear or confusion---and or desire for safety or love): "Yes, I said it was alright to beat me," or "Yes, I asked for it. My being beaten is my fault."*

ASK DR. ANGELA
#701: Emotional and Physical Abuse in Relationships, Part One

Let's dig a bit deeper into the muddle we call consent. Explicit consent is generally viewed as being expressed directly by means of spoken or written agreement. Implied consent is somewhat more obscure, as it is generally viewed as being expressed indirectly, through actions or behaviors that give the suggestion or appearance of consent. Implied consent is risky.

In instances of implied consent, partners should seek clear, explicit, actual mutual consent after dialoging about what this actually means. *If all parties belonging to the intimate partner relationship have not fully, clearly, and explicitly consented to something, then full consent has not been given for that something.*

The complexity and elusive nature of abuse and violence in relationships is manifested in issues of intent and consent. So, let's step back here and look from another angle at this animal—at this life form—we call the intimate partner relationship....

ASK DR. ANGELA® SERIES
ASK DR. ANGELA About Intimate and Other Partner
Abuse and Violence

ASK DR. ANGELA
#701: Emotional and Physical
Abuse in Relationships, Part One

Chapter 7
Power Difference Story

When she married John twenty years ago, Cathy had no idea what her future held. She and John were in love.

From the start, there appeared to be an "almost charming" power difference (and <u>power differential</u>, although the differential aspect, which included shifting power issues over time, was not understood yet). This power difference seemed to be the result of Cathy being significantly younger than John, as well as earlier in her career.

As the years progressed and they had children, the choices they made tended to be in support of John's career as his earning power was higher than Cathy's. And, his earning power remained higher for various reasons including choices not to relocate for Cathy's career; to have Cathy stay at home with the children when they were young; to have Cathy put her career second to John's and the family; and to not look closely at what was taking place all along the way. All this made sense to John and Cathy. They believed in nurturing the family and closely attending to the children (while having which ever parent could bring home the largest paycheck out more hours earning that paycheck).

What did not make sense, and was never discussed between them during the first decade of their marriage, was the emerging of abuse and violence in their relationship. At first, this violence was sporadic, but over time it grew habitual and responded to triggers very much like substance (e.g., alcohol, drug, and nicotine) addiction can.

ASK DR. ANGELA® SERIES
ASK DR. ANGELA About Intimate and Other Partner Abuse and Violence

Looking back much later (and extending the understanding of physical violence to verbal and gestured threats of violence, damaging of items or pets around or near a person, and light pushing and shoving during arguments), neither Cathy nor John can recall the first time the violence took place.

Yet, in increments, the violence escalated, and Cathy suffered several injuries along the way, all of which she told her friends and family were the result of falls and her lack of coordination. She and John both hid the truth about the domestic violence from others and from themselves.

The problem grew worse and Cathy's injuries more extreme. Neighbors, friends, and relatives were increasingly suspicious, and at least some eventually certain, that there was a problem. Eventually, Cathy and John were unable to hide what was happening from their children, who had actually known all along.

Cathy herself, some fourteen years into the marriage, began calling the police about John's violence. However, when the police would arrive, Cathy would be afraid of both social stigma and John's retribution and would say it had been a prowler. The more often Cathy said this to the police, the more they questioned her credibility.

Of course, right to the end—when John had broken Cathy's arm, bruised and cut her face so much she could not cover it up with makeup, knocked out her tooth, and split her lip—when Cathy finally realized John actually could someday kill her and therefore moved out—there were times when John was not only apologetic but even romantic. He loved Cathy very much, she was everything to him, he continued to tell her.

ASK DR. ANGELA
#701: Emotional and Physical Abuse in Relationships, Part One

Cathy, who had gone into the marriage with the strong belief that this was a lifelong commitment, was reluctant to leave, yet, when she finally did, she did not want to go back. She actually felt safe for the first time in almost two decades. Yet, this safety was not long lived, as John began stalking her and intruding without warning into her new residence, claiming to desperately miss her and the children.

Eventually, Cathy turned to the court to get restraining orders keeping John away. The entire process was heart breaking as she loved John very much. Furthermore, the children, now older but still wanting the family intact, were also broken hearted.

Yet, once away from it long enough to see clearly, Cathy realized how much she wanted to stop being verbally and physically abused and threatened, and hit and beaten. Only when she was out of the marriage did she realize how very much she wanted her freedom from this troubled relationship, and its painful and dangerous patterns.

The problem was that Cathy felt more in danger now . . . .

ASK DR. ANGELA® SERIES
ASK DR. ANGELA About Intimate and Other Partner Abuse and Violence

ASK DR. ANGELA
#701: Emotional and Physical
Abuse in Relationships, Part One

Chapter 8
Precious Time

You wait to make a change. You wait for the strength, or for a sign, or for the way to change. Wait and wait and wait. But there seems to be no right time. And there seems to be no time to change the way you relate to each other. Years race by, and then years are gone.

You cannot get those years back. Yet you can be ever more conscious of how you relate from this point on.

It has been said time and again:

> *It is very important
> with whom you choose
> to spend the time of your life.*

Yes, it is very important, and who would say otherwise.

TIME PASSES NO MATTER WHAT

Of few things we are certain, and one of these things is that time passes. Before we know it, days, weeks, months, years, and even decades have sped by like grains of sand slipping through our fingers. This is a key message, the importance of which is difficult to express to the young for whom time may seem abundant. It is typically only after many many years that the gravity of this message is felt. Looking back is easy enough to do. We see so much more with 20-20 hindsight.

ASK DR. ANGELA® SERIES
ASK DR. ANGELA About Intimate and Other Partner Abuse and Violence

Yet, do we actually know so much more after the fact?

What could we do differently if we could turn back the hands of time? Anything? Anything at all? Yes, we could and now can do **more conscious relating**.

CAN WE CHOOSE CAREFULLY

Taking care to choose carefully who we spend the time of our lives with…. This is not a very profound concept; in fact, at first glance, this makes complete sense. Sounds easy. We even may hear about this all too often. So we may say, of course, we are careful about who we choose to spend our precious time with! Yes! Yes?

Yet, in the early stages of relationships, especially when we are young, such a question is not only considered to be irrelevant but also inconvenient, even intrusive. Especially when physical sexual attraction is mingled with the emotion we tend to call "in love," our emotional and physical biochemistries color any discussion of the importance of how we choose a partner.

"Don't bother me with such a downer, with such a silly concept. If I weren't very much wanting to spend the time of my life with this person—to spend every second I possibly can with this person—this person I AM IN LOVE WITH—then of course I wouldn't, duh."

And then, if the relationship flowers into the commitments it can bring—marriage, family, and all that goes with it—these signal to the outside world (such as friends, extended family, neighbors, co-workers, the boss)—that what is good to think

ASK DR. ANGELA
#701: Emotional and Physical Abuse in Relationships, Part One

about is being thought about.

Of course, for the few who then form troubled relationships, thinking about all this may be after the fact, a little bit late to be considering carefully who you want to spend the time of your life with. You're already spending it! You're right in the middle of the process! The few who then find they need to make a change learn that any unraveling of this commitment takes work and often can mean divorce. Divorce itself can be emotionally, physically, and financially costly for the couple as well as for others nearby, such as the children. Yet for some there is no choice.

For many, there are choices every step of the way through staying, and through staying over time. And of course, many years, even decades, into the process, long after the kids are grown, long after the first grandchild has been born, when you are finally able to look back and realize how very important it is to think carefully about who you spend the time of your life with, you have already done it—or tried. Precious years have gone by. So make these years good.

Might there be another process which could allow for greater care in selection? We must ask....

Our grandparents and great grandparents, and or other ancestors, may have said so and may even have wanted a say in choosing our mates. This procedure may have guaranteed happiness somewhat more than the mail order bride process. But can it work in our rapidly changing times? Probably not in most cases.

Still, given the high present day divorce rate, who can say which mate selection procedure creates the greatest chance of lifelong satisfaction with one's significant-other-intimate-partner relationship? (This book can and does say: ***try consciously forming relationships and conscious relating all along***.) Certainly, lifelong satisfaction with a relationship is subjective. Satisfaction means different things to different people.

To some extent, complete or near complete satisfaction with one's primary relationship is a luxury few can demand. Simply surviving, having a roof over one's head and food on the table, is already success. And this important element of sheer survival must never be overlooked, especially where children are involved. *Should we want more than this out of life? Can we afford to want more? What do we risk when we want more?*

CHOICE, SURVIVAL, AND FINANCES

While love drives many marriages, we must also see that some marriages are formed and then stay together for economic reasons. Some marriages are formed based upon the perceived earning power or present or future wealth of a mate or of both mates. Some troubled marriages may even remain in place (or have to remain in place) simply because of one mate's economic dependence upon another, others simply because both mates find the cost of living more affordable when sharing the cost, and others simply because the cost of divorce appears prohibitive. (Not all of these choices are signs of trouble. Many of these choices may make sense.)

ASK DR. ANGELA
#701: Emotional and Physical Abuse in Relationships, Part One

CONTROL OVER MONEY

That there is an economic element to marriage and coupling is not in itself a crime. If business partnerships form, at least in part, for economic reasons, why not love, intimate, casual, and similar partnerships? Let's face it, the business of sharing lives, of sharing costs, responsibilities, and chores, is a business. Even a merging of lives, a coupling or a marriage, especially when there are, or will be, children, is an economic relationship.

So, the question is, can we mix love and the business of life successfully? Can we avoid opportunities for the abuse of this love-plus-economic relationship as it is being formed, and all through its years of existence? Yes, of course. (*Note that even after its existence, if there is a break-up, divorce, etc., the* **post-relationship relationship** *is definitely still a relationship, and can, and too frequently does, continue or even exaggerate risks of abuse and violence in relationships where those risks already existed prior to the break-up.*)

In businesses, control over the books, the spending, and the money itself, is organized in such a way that the business can survive and even thrive. The organization of this control is indeed designed to help the business survive and thrive. The logical parallel in couples and families is that this same control, although more informal, is designed to help the partnership and the family survive and thrive. In most couple relationships, of course, the organization of control over finances is not as straightforward as it is in businesses. Instead, much of it is casual, even ad hoc.

ASK DR. ANGELA® SERIES
ASK DR. ANGELA About Intimate and Other Partner Abuse and Violence

However, many modern relationship partners do rise to the challenge of clearly and mutually managing, and communicating about, their money.

Of course, love and control over money are not necessarily natural bedfellows. When control of money is lopsided, control in the relationship can (but does not always) become lopsided as well.

It is frequently best that a marriage or similar relationship's money management be done together by the relationship partners. And where this is not possible or wanted, then next best is at least a very complete and ongoing communication with each other about money. Couples deciding who will have what responsibility for managing the money they make, save, and spend will do well to take great care to watch that this management does not distort (in a way that could disadvantage one or both partners) the balanced and fair power structure of this relationship.

As we all know, power unchecked, unmonitored, does not always but indeed can allow the abuse of power. All too often, when one member of a couple controls more of the financial reality than the other, there is room for that controlling member to have some power which the other does not have, even if this is merely decision-making or information-based power.

A few are tempted to take advantage of this power, to engage in financial abuse. Most choose the positive alternative: equal access to, and equal information regarding, the couple's finances and related financial information. This may be the

ASK DR. ANGELA
#701: Emotional and Physical Abuse in Relationships, Part One

best approach for relationship partners. This is not only healthy, this reduces chances of financial confusion and or abuse.

THE WAY IT SHOULD BE

Clearly, relationship building and maintenance is not a simple undertaking. It is easier for many to just do it and to avoid delving into what is happening while they are doing it. And, there is a strong social directive to just do it, saying: just have a relationship, don't look too closely, don't question the process.

Indeed, there are those who will say, "this is how it is supposed to be" and "that's life." Recall the old adage:

[So and so], sitting in a tree, K-I-S-S-I-N-G. First comes love, then comes marriage. Then comes the baby in the baby carriage.

This picture—love then marriage then baby—slips into many young minds as early as the nursery rhyme stage of life, forming a sort of directive, a norm which young people come to feel is most acceptable and most normal.

But what if this is not how it is supposed to be? Or what if this is not how it is supposed to be in this day and age? Or perhaps supposed to be, yet is nowhere as simple as nursery rhymes suggest....

This norm is in reality so complex that while it is transmitted from generation to generation via nursery rhymes, fairy tales, spoken expectations, movies, and modeling done by older generations, no one can say what all goes into it.

No one can say for sure that this is truly "how it is supposed to be" or exactly what all it is that is supposed to be. No one can promise that good and wonderful experiences are normal in, and can be expected of, this sort of supposed to be arrangement. Nor can anyone say comfortably in our time that the abuse and violence which can take place in some of these arrangements is alright, part of the plan.

It is up to the members of the relationship to maintain a healthy relationship—to regularly communicate with themselves on a mutual, ongoing, and open basis.

CHOOSING WHEN THERE ARE UNKNOWNS

There is so much to be discovered about ourselves and our partners, that we cannot see this all up front. Years and years of discovery may not reveal even the majority of what there is to know. Instead, we must be sensitive to how our relationships play out or evolve over time.

We must be attentive to signs—signs of positive and neutral, and also of negative, trends—within ourselves, our partners, and our relationships. We must be conscious of what is taking place, rather than turn a blind eye (as discussed in upcoming chapters).

Most relationships go quite well. Yet, some people miss early signs of potential future abuse and violence. Even where conscious steps into a relationship are taken, relationship partners do best to always remain in the conscious state.

ASK DR. ANGELA
#701: Emotional and Physical
Abuse in Relationships, Part One

Chapter 9
Cherish is a Word For

To have and to hold, to cherish, until death do us part, are wordings typical of many traditional marriage vows. What goes into taking these vows or other more modern vows? What do these words mean to us while speaking them, and years after?

HOW WE CHERISH EACH OTHER

Cherish. What does it mean to "cherish"? Do we know? Do we know how to cherish? To have and to hold, to cherish, has been a popular ideal transmitted to young people (and others of all ages for that matter) thinking about marriage.

That we frequently hear this cherishing, or something like this, as a value expressed in wedding vows is to some people perhaps a little unclear. Yet clarity is not exactly what the vow is about—or is it? Most people taking marriage vows have, at the time they take them, no precise idea what it is they are promising in real life and real-time terms, and do not wonder much.

And knowing what cherishing is all about comes with time, is written in our hearts and minds as we learn about it.

This is alright, because it has to be alright, because love is so kindly blind. When deeply in love, it can be difficult to see, let alone want to see, nitty-gritty aspects of reality. In fact,

ASK DR. ANGELA® SERIES
ASK DR. ANGELA About Intimate and Other Partner Abuse and Violence

love is a delightful state of mind, heart, and body, a state which is largely biochemical and hormonal. Fortunately, many modern adults understand this and are taking far more interest in consciously dialoging with their future partners.

The dance between and among one's own (personal) biochemistries, and the various interpersonal biochemistries one is engaging in and interacting with, is complex, and largely taking place out of our conscious awareness. Yet this complex biochemical dance is triggered by, and also triggering, so much around and within us--and most certainly also in our relationships.

Love is a sort of drug, and response to love can be lovely. Yet for some, there can be an addiction-like involvement with the processes of cherishing and being in love. This should not be too surprising. For some people in love, this is what it means to cherish: to be addicted body, mind, and soul (and heart) to another person. Of course, this is not the definition of cherish. Yet cherish too often gets played out this way. (And of course, many addictions are quite healthy. Still, it is wise to watch for troubles in even positive habit and addiction patterns as these can at times run awry without our noticing.[4])

It is up to each of us to look closely and honestly at ourselves and at our own forms of loving, and of feeling loved.

---

[4] See the books where I have explained in depth my work in areas of emotional, behavioral, relationship, and also alcohol/drug use patterns, habits, and addictions, such as the book, *SEEING THE HIDDEN FACE OF ADDICTION*, and also the *NAVIGATING LIFE'S STUFF* books. See the reading list at the end of this present book.

ASK DR. ANGELA
#701: Emotional and Physical Abuse in Relationships, Part One

WHEN IS CHERISH CONFUSION OR EVEN DECEPTION?

What it feels like to cherish and to be cherished can be confused and muddled. We can fool ourselves about our being cherished, and about what this means.

We can think we are cherishing and are being cherished when we are not. After all, do we really know what cherish looks like? Cherish is not a fixation, an addiction, or an obsession. Nor is the act of cherishing itself the sacrifice of one's life to someone else's will "out of love and dedication."

Nor is the presence of cherishing in a relationship itself a dominance and submission arrangement. Yet, the sense that one is being cherished by her or his partner may confuse matters. Not only is the cherishing itself unclear, what takes place and at times is even confused by the sense that cherishing is taking place, can at times allow for abuse.

WHEN ABUSE OF DOMINANCE HIDES BEHIND LOVE AND CHERISH LABELS

A note about dominance here. Here, dominance is related to the *organization of power and control* in the relationship. (Elsewhere in these books, I have noted that many relationships efficiently and fairly delegate responsibilities and even control of particular jobs key in maintaining the homes and lives of the members of the relationship. Not all dominance is abused, and quite often, dominance is fairly divided in terms of who will take on what job for the good of them both.)

ASK DR. ANGELA® SERIES
ASK DR. ANGELA About Intimate and Other Partner Abuse and Violence

In instances where one partner dominates and controls some or all of the other partner's space and safety, and also perhaps business, assets, time, choices, arrangements, and or decisions, the power and control this dominance offers may in some cases be abused.

Against the backdrop of love and trust, of cherishing one's partner, abuse can arise, even sneak in. Where emotional abuse (such as that described in the last chapter of this book) is present, the abuse of power and control can augment the underlying abuse situation.

Note: At times, this less visible yet quite dangerous level of abuse can be undetected while doing great harm. Some relationships move into realms of serious harm, long before the harm that is already taking place fully registers. (*As noted several times in this book, the long term consequences of abuse and violence in a relationship may become clear long after the relationship is over, when the harm that has been caused becomes more clear and the damages more apparent.*)

In instances of intimate partner abuse and violence, (IPAV), the dominant partner may also be, in essence, engaging in a more twisted, convoluted, vaguely sadistic process. Here, the dominant partner abusively administers onto the other partner suppression, fear, harm, and or pain. The abusive dominant partner may even say or imply that this abuse is being administered at the supposed request of the other partner. The workings of the undercurrent of abuse of dominance in a relationship may not reveal themselves until years later when the harm caused is still more apparent. (See the following books, *#702, #703, and #704*.)

ASK DR. ANGELA
#701: Emotional and Physical
Abuse in Relationships, Part One

THIS IS NOT ABOUT
A PARENT CHILD DOMINANCE

Keep in mind that this discussion of dominance, of power and control in a relationship, does not apply to all relationships, and does not say all power and control, or even dominance, is being abused. In fact, much dominance, and even power in control in relating, is necessary. The greatest example of this is in parenting and family organization. Where there are natural dependents such as children, parents have a responsibility to maintain their dominance, to exercise control, in healthy ways.

This book is not talking about parent child relationships where the children are dependents.

This book is, however, talking about some
actual adult relationships which sometimes
mistakenly, inadvertently, or perhaps at times even purposefully
confuse themselves with parent–child relationships...
...in which one member is
somehow in charge of the other
and has ultimate say, either intentionally or unintentionally
...and or one member is or appears to be
more dependent upon the other.

This dynamic must be consciously understood so that the members
of the relationship are aware of the dynamic,
*the **power flow** within the relationship.*

ASK DR. ANGELA® SERIES
ASK DR. ANGELA About Intimate and Other Partner Abuse and Violence

WHEN CHERISH IS A LICENSE TO HAVE

When is marriage, or any intimate partner relationship, more a license simply to have, and even sometimes to have the sad way: to have and to sometimes hurt, to do whatever good or harm comes about?

What elements of this issue are important for all of us, whether or not experiencing problem relationships? Why are these important?

It is all too easy to slip into a painful situation without seeing that this is happening. It is all too easy to then continue not seeing that this is happening while remaining unaware of this situation for a lifetime, or for a long time, or at least until it begins to hurt so much that we have to notice it.

Yes, sometimes a person <u>adapts to being abused</u>.

Experiencing abuse can then seem "normal" and become virtually normalized. The reverse can also be true: sometimes a person adapts to abusING. AbusING can also then seem "normal" and become virtually normalized.

Thank goodness not all relationships follow this deteriorating route. Most do not! Still, some relationships are at risk of this.

And every relationship can benefit from a **preventive awareness** *of this dangerous tendency to not realize something is deteriorating a little until it has deteriorated a great deal.*

ASK DR. ANGELA
#701: Emotional and Physical Abuse in Relationships, Part One

ELEMENT OF OWNERSHIP

The notion of *partner ownership* is, in most settings and societies, seemingly not relevant. However, look again. Subtle aspects of *ownership of another* may seep in without partners realizing this is taking place. Perhaps this is the sense that one partner "owns" the other's time, choices, reputation, body, reproductive functioning, and so on.

Indeed, sometimes an element of, or form of, this **partner ownership** does enter a relationship—even when undetected by both parties. When this happens there can be an eroding of the *equal voice, value and say* found in healthy relationships.

When this even vague partner ownership enters a relationship, the processes of cherishing and accepting each other can become quite complex, sometimes even convoluted.

What is being traded or agreed to in effort to maintain the relationship? Do the members of the relationship actually know? Do they know the difference between the individual's boundaries and the relationship's boundaries?

Do they understand that abuse of a partner for the supposed sake of the relationship is not boundary respect? Do they see the difference between boundary respect and boundary trespassing (trespassing where subtle yet very present partner abuse and ownership tendencies can surface)?

A relationship's boundaries can be well protected and respected without degrees of partner boundary trespassing and subtle forms of partner ownership. Yet sometimes people

ASK DR. ANGELA® SERIES
ASK DR. ANGELA About Intimate and Other Partner Abuse and Violence

get these confused. *Sometimes one partner feels <u>entitled</u> to cross the other partner's boundaries,* **feels a sense of ownership of this entitlement or supposed right.**

The notion that one person can own another (or can own the right to cross another person's boundaries without that person's informed and freely given permission) may sound wrong or old fashioned. Yet this idea, or attitude, can sneak up on partners in runaway, addictive, and or obsessive partnerships—and also on partners in healthier relationships.

As incorrect and rare as this ownership tendency may sound, partners in relationships must be aware that subtle forms of this can appear in many interactions without people seeing it.

Yes…this ownership dynamic
can slip into a relationship almost unnoticed.
Ownership tendencies
can even be
vague, difficult to spot, in some cases.

Whether or not ownership is too strong a word for most situations, the **notion of <u>entitlement to control</u> is part of this ownership concept.**

Partners must know that they can participate in exchanges in which one person takes over, whether (a) without the other's consent, or (b) with the other's full consent, or (c) with the other fooling her or him self into **not-seeing** this happening, or (d) with the other truly **not-seeing** this happening—*not-seeing this happening until it is too late to prevent this (even where there is abuse of power and control emerging).* (Note that this verb

ASK DR. ANGELA
#701: Emotional and Physical Abuse in Relationships, Part One

defined in this book, this *not-seeing*, takes on a particular nature of its own. This is the *act of* NOT-seeing, which will be referred to several times in this book, *#701, and in the following books in this series, ASK DR. ANGELA #702 and #703.*)

TINY TRADES

Many minor, almost unnoticed interactions take place during a relationship. For the most part, we do not focus on these exchanges and do not see their actual nature. Most of these exchanges and interactions are lovely, or at least useful, functional, and or too minor to spot.

Let's return for a moment to the concept of *equal partnering*. Here, two consenting adults cherish each other as equal partners, of *equal respect, voice, value, and say*, in their relationship. For many, this is the standard by which they measure—or at least feel—the successes of their relationships, and this is good. Yet, applying this standard is easier said than done for some.

The equality standard is all too often oversimplified to absurdity. Expecting people, even partners in relationships, to actually be exactly the same and equal in every way is irrational and denies the value of individuality. Each of us has our own set of personal characteristics, and nothing says we are or should be exact copies of each other in appearance, behavior, performance, taste, or belief system.

Equal partnering is not about pretending or talking like we are all exactly the same or equal in every way. It is about allowing, promoting, and desiring equal levels of importance and power in a partnership—fairly distributing respect, voice, value, and say in the business and personal interactions of the relationship.

Even when trying, this model of equal voice, value, and say in relationship takes attention. No matter how much we think we have arranged ourselves in such a way that everything is done in an atmosphere of equal respect, voice, value, and say, there are many hidden trades that take place almost every day and sometimes almost every minute of a relationship.

Each time there is an interaction, there is a choice to feel, say, or do—or not to feel, say, or do—something, a passage in time in which one or the other puts either the relationship first, the partner first, or the self first. While each of these choices can be admirable or at least normal, just know that each of these times, there is a tiny transaction taking place.

These transactions are not in themselves sources of pain, and they can be navigated with sensitivity and appreciation for the process of balancing the give and take required to keep a relationship functional and happy.

Many couples achieve this sort of balance without working hard to do so, and this is ultimately the goal where possible.

At the same time, some couples never reach this balance. Then, as time goes by, they trap themselves or at least one of their members into ongoing chiseling away at or sacrificing of self—and of stability, sanity, and safety.

ASK DR. ANGELA
#701: Emotional and Physical Abuse in Relationships, Part One

It is then that the vows some couples, just some but indeed some, take can be distorted into traps, licenses to cause pain, hurt, and damage—not because the vows say this but because the vows can be misused, misinterpreted, misunderstood either intentionally or unintentionally.

Two consenting adults can choose to cherish each other as equal partners, with equal respect, voice, value, and say in their relationship. Try to check around. See what various couples say about this….

POWER DIFFERENTIALS

The deck of opportunity is rarely evenly dealt out or shared. Distributions of careers, good jobs, incomes, and other chances to live up to one's potential and or to fulfill one's dreams are uneven enough in this world.

However, in a coupling relationship—even in a loving one fully aware of the issues relating to opportunities and what is sometimes given up by one or both of the relationship members—given up or set aside for each other and or for the family over time—this "giving up" or "setting aside" of opportunity can have long term effects.

What starts out simple—two people coming together based on attraction and love, and perhaps shared dreams, and then *not-seeing* how their differences can be magnified over time— can grow messy where couples do not stay conscious of choices and trades being made every step of the way.

ASK DR. ANGELA® SERIES
ASK DR. ANGELA About Intimate and Other Partner Abuse and Violence

Conscious approaches to the interactions taking place from the start can help prevent unintentional confusion and upset. These can help spot the early warning signs of slight and easily addressed issues, and also the possible signs of budding emotional, financial, and other forms of abuse and violence.

It is in the little steps that some vague, confusing, challenging, sometimes even wrong, even rocky, directions are sometimes taken.

Look before you leap, and walk with awareness and respect for each other and yourselves. This awareness and respect can be a healthy part of a loving relationship. This can make a big difference in the long run.

ASK DR. ANGELA
#701: Emotional and Physical
Abuse in Relationships, Part One

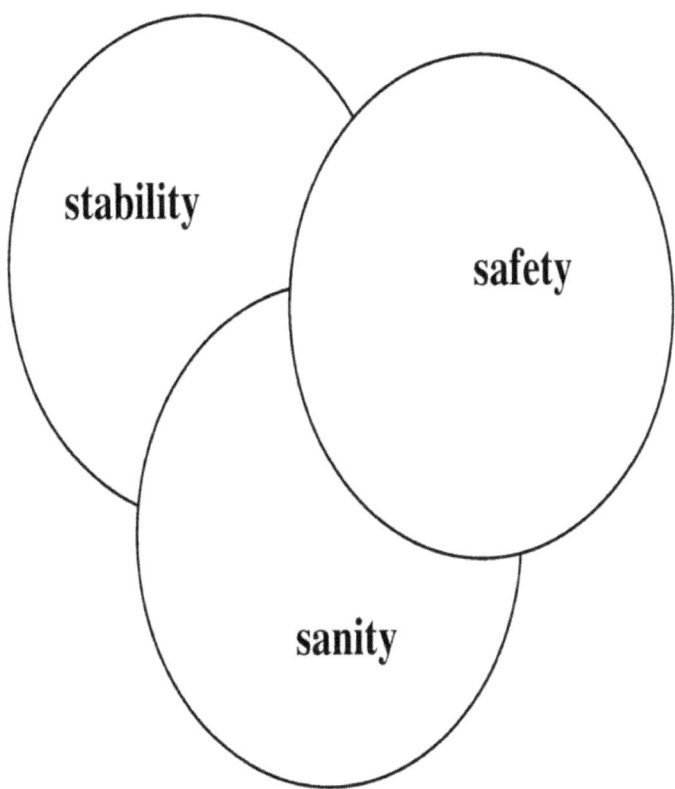

Figure 9.1. Stability, sanity, and safety balance.

ASK DR. ANGELA® SERIES
ASK DR. ANGELA About Intimate and Other Partner Abuse and Violence

ASK DR. ANGELA
#701: Emotional and Physical
Abuse in Relationships, Part One

Chapter 10
Second Thought Story

She had heard about these wedding jitters, these bouts of nervousness and restlessness, possibly even craziness, in the weeks, days, and hours before some people's weddings. But never had she even considered the possibility that those jitters she was experiencing could in any way be actual second thoughts.

She simply attributed her engaging in several short, wild, and nearly anonymous affairs, sexual escapades, in other cities where no one knew her, to normal anxiety which would pass.

At least, she told herself, this kind of behavior was acceptable for men right before marriage. So, she asked herself, why not for women, too? After all, she thought, "tying the knot" had a slightly binding sound to it, a disturbingly permanent sound to it, a bit like a guillotine about to fall with everyone watching and giving full consent to the termination of her freedom.

She kept herself busy to avoid wondering whether marrying a man she had known for only four months, whose baby she was now carrying, made sense.

She reassured herself that the wedding vows would make it all OK.

ASK DR. ANGELA® SERIES
ASK DR. ANGELA About Intimate and Other Partner Abuse and Violence

ASK DR. ANGELA
#701: Emotional and Physical
Abuse in Relationships, Part One

Chapter 11
Individual Identity and Boundaries Within A Relationship

For those who are, or ever have been, deeply in love, a celebration of this love and of the mutual commitments to it can be a wonderfully joyous event. This celebration is a wedding of lives and for many, one of the biggest events in their lives, a peak experience. As one of the high points in life, the positive aspects of being together and committing to share lives have to be acknowledged, respected, and protected. For many, this is a precious rite of passage.

NOTICE OF BONDING

Yet, for a range of reasons, there exists for some, for not all yet for some, a great deal of anxiety about relationship commitment let alone marriage. One of the unspoken aspects of this anxiety has to do with the shift in personal identity that merging lives may bring some people.

Some find this an increase in and a solidification of personal identity, in that marrying or establishing a primary relationship *can be the maturation of self and the achievement of a major lifetime goal. And this is fabulous.*

Others, however, are uncertain as to what the effects of this merging of lives with another person will have upon their own identities. Rarely is it admitted by those with identity issues that these nagging questions are swimming just below the surface, and rarely do they dare to openly ask:

"Will I lose myself in you," or,
"Will you be taking my life over," or,
"Will I be myself anymore," or even,
"Is this a very good idea, as I do not even know who I am."

Yet, there is nothing wrong with openly asking these questions if these are there to be asked. Even discussing these issues whether or not these questions are recognized can be useful. Why not talk about these things if they are lurking in the under currents of one or both partners' thinking? Partners can find safe ways to discuss all of this.

WHEN A BOND CROSSES THE LINE

The wedding or other formalizing of the partnership of love is an explicit notice of what social scientists have called pair-bonding. This wedding of persons is a positive form of formal human bond, a formal bond of love and likely mating. In some ways, like two companies merging, there is frequently a formal written or spoken agreement signifying the intent of the parties to combine or partner in some way. For many intimate partners, the spoken agreement comes in the form of formal wedding and or civil partnership vows, while the license, and for some, the marital agreement, is written and even certified.

All partnerships in love can protect their love by being open and honest with each other (and with themselves). These intimate partner relationships and their members best travel

ASK DR. ANGELA
#701: Emotional and Physical
Abuse in Relationships, Part One

the journey of love, and of relating, with great awareness, care, and respect. The pair bond is a bond that requires highly conscious nurturing and protecting to be an ongoing healthy and positive bond.

It is wise to understand that this bond can sometimes cross a line, sometimes through no fault of anyone's, just because life is like this. This line or boundary crossing can be addressed wisely and well, and worked with as it takes place.

Sometimes members of a relationship move beyond a line or boundary without the *full awareness and agreement of both members of the relationship*. There can be risks for these relationships and the partners within these relationships. Yes, past this line are risks, as past this line are potentially dangerous territories. Where partners do not fully see what they are agreeing to do (or not to do) with their own lives for the sake of their relationship, they risk boundary and identity confusion. They can of course ward this off by bringing as much as they can into the light of conscious choice, and conscious behavior, and conscious interaction.

Otherwise, the relationship bond can become more of an agreement to hold one or both partners in a form of **bond**-age, bondage to the relationship and or to each other. Yes, this bondage is fine where partners are consciously and explicitly aware of their contributions and agreements all along the way. Then this can be a healthy choice for all involved.

Where partners are unaware of the full scope of their relationship agreements, and of their own personal as well as their relationship's identity and boundary definitions, they leave the rules and structure of their relationship vague, ambiguous, and potentially or actually unstable.

Ambiguity in itself is a problem which is generally so ambiguous that it goes on unrecognized while generating relationship confusion and shakiness. Potential and actual destabilizing and deterioration of the relationship can result.

The art of seeing this ambiguous problem of ambiguity coming before it manifests itself is worth studying. Alas, this is not a recognized art. What would we call this?

> *Positive bond protection?*
> *Protection from deterioration into…*
> > *an unclear, confusing form of*
> > > *relating, perhaps even bondage?*

REASONS FOR FORMAL MARRIAGE

History has evolved marriage ceremonying and licensing for several reasons, among these being that marriage has offered:

- A way to transfer ownership of property (and of women and children in eras and settings where they were legally defined as property, chattel, along with money, land, livestock, and other material things).
- A way to protect property, whatever this property may be.

ASK DR. ANGELA
#701: Emotional and Physical Abuse in Relationships, Part One

- A way to indicate, mark, the parentage and lineage of children.
- A way to signify that two persons' sexual intercourse is or was socially acceptable.
- A way to make sexual intercourse and any children it would bring legally and religiously acceptable and "legitimate."
- A way to protect children produced by the union.

Marriage vows have evolved along with marriage and even today can contain implicit and explicit references to commitment, ownership, and property. Both religious and secular versions of the old "to have and to hold" vow continue to be popular. These tend to include phrases such as "for better or for worse" and "for richer, for poorer, in sickness and in health."

These are beautiful and profound commitments. The question here is, are these vows fully understood when they are being taken?

Some vows continue to include or imply an "until death do us part" term as well. The basic message is that "nothing will tear us apart" and "we are committed to this union from this day forward." Permanency and strength of the bond are being promised. And this is good, otherwise, (one might ask) why formalize this bond?

ASK DR. ANGELA® SERIES
ASK DR. ANGELA About Intimate and Other Partner Abuse and Violence

IDENTITY AND COMMITMENT TO WHAT AND TO WHOM

And why not make such promises? Isn't lifelong commitment most often viewed as being the point of the marriage? And why not make such a promise formal and public? Isn't the promise made to not only the partner, but to any future (or existing) offspring and to the community as well? These guarantees are statements of what the community surrounding the couple, and all couples in this community, can expect of those taking the vow.

There is of course a strong ceremonial aspect to the sharing of vows done by couples. Sharing of vows becomes an event, a ritual, a reason for celebration, and frequently publicly marks what would otherwise be a very private rite of passage taking place. This ceremony can serve as official, social, and spiritual approval, authorization, and permission for the union of lives, bodies, families, and property that is taking place. And this is usually a deeply meaningful and beautiful ceremony.

Union, yes. Now two individuals unite, and in some ways of seeing it, become one. However, they actually become at least three: two individuals plus one relationship—or plus the relationship each of them thinks he or she is entering—which may make it at least four. Yes, four: two individuals plus the relationship which each sees there. And this is before adding on additional perceptions each member of the couple has of the other member of the couple. "I am marrying the person I think you are." And this is before any children are added on.

ASK DR. ANGELA
#701: Emotional and Physical Abuse in Relationships, Part One

(While some relationships do include more than the two members of the couple, this discussion refers to the couple and to the pair bond as this is the most common form of primary intimate partner relationship. Readers who wish to extend this information to other forms of relationships will do so with whatever adaptations of this information are involved to do so.)

Marriage is a vessel of transmission for a culture. When the marriage is an officially "approved" marriage, legally and for many also religiously accepted, then the culture in which the marriage is performed approves of the marriage. This culture thus makes this marriage an important component of itself, of this culture, and of the process of this culture's continuation and preservation.

Note that little about the institution of marriage is truly aimed at continuation and preservation of the individual. Not exactly anyway. *This remains up to the people getting married.*

Times change, and modern times are changing ever more rapidly. Old values and concepts are being reexamined and in some arenas heavily questioned.

If relationships, love partnerships, couplings, and marriages do not evolve, they may not survive the evolution of the societies where they live. The reverse is also true: societies must keep up with the relationships being formed within them!

So must we all.

ASK DR. ANGELA® SERIES
ASK DR. ANGELA About Intimate and Other Partner Abuse and Violence

ASK DR. ANGELA
#701: Emotional and Physical
Abuse in Relationships, Part One

Chapter 12
Meet the IP's Boundary

Although many do, not all relationship partners marry, or bond for life or for years. Some relationships are brief and casual, some are not, yet many may still be flexible and undefined in duration. Either way, once there is emotional or physical intimacy, or both, there is a meshing of or blurring of boundaries.

Intimacy is shared boundary crossing with mutual permission and invitation. To be clear here: The opposite of intimacy is boundary crossing without permission and without invitation, in essence a violation, a sort of raping of a boundary, of a person's boundary, of a person's self.

Certainly sex or physical intimacy appears to be intimate. Standing naked before each other, we appear to ourselves and each other to be truly naked, and we feel naked. So naked. Yet, we really are just doing some boundary shedding and boundary crossing. How easy it is to feel that this is intimate.

Most physical intimacy is wanted by both partners (is clearly mutually agreed upon), and is a positive experience for both partners. Where not, partners do best by knowing this, as this is an area where transgressions of oneself, and or of the partner, are possible even when both think they are being sensitive to boundaries.

ASK DR. ANGELA® SERIES
ASK DR. ANGELA About Intimate and Other Partner Abuse and Violence

Intimacy is central in many relationships, hence the label "intimate" partner relationship (IPV). It is generally assumed that this term "intimacy" refers to sexual intimacy, however this is not the only form of intimacy in relationships.

INTIMACY IS NOT PHYSICAL NAKEDNESS

Intimacy is indeed far more than only physical. Intimacy reaches well beyond people being physically naked together. In fact, sexual relations may or may not result in any degree of emotional intimacy whatsoever. So, who, other than someone you may get naked with and may have sex with, is the intimate partner? Anyone? Yes, however look closely before answering.

You may have had several persons you would call intimate partners, several who have once qualified or still do qualify. Many readers will have selected one of these, or are in the process of doing so. This is likely the spouse, life partner, significant other, although these labels do not actually capture the deep, interwoven, nature of the relationship we are talking about.

(Some readers will have a primary life partner and another intimate partner outside of that primary relationship. Where this book does not evaluate choices to or not to do so, again the emphasis here is on <u>mutual and fully informed agreements</u> by <u>both</u> partners in the primary relationship. Where there are not mutual conscious agreements by both members of a relationship, there can be or already is boundary crossing and therefore a form of abuse taking place.

ASK DR. ANGELA
#701: Emotional and Physical Abuse in Relationships, Part One

Consider as example a situation where one partner believes the relationship is monogamous, and where the other partner is not monogamous. This is likely not mutual and explicitly informed consent on the part of both partners. One partner is likely lying to the other. Why would both partners not have a right to be fully informed that their relationship is not monogamous? This is not a discussion regarding extramarital affairs. This is however a note regarding mutual consent. Is the absence of mutual consent while proceeding without mutual consent an opening to abuse?[5]

ENTANGLEMENT IS NOT INTIMACY

Let's not let this description, "deep and entangled," paint an entirely negative picture. Many highly functional, natural, and very good things are deep and entangled such as: rich positive relationships, fertile beds of seaweed, and neural networks in the human brain. Still, it is in this deep entangled way that entanglement can bind us, that it can allow us to think a deeply entangled intimate partner relationship is an intimate one.

---

[5] One instance where this question arose was where one member of a marriage contracted HIV while he was having an extramarital affair, while he was not informing the other member of the marriage, his wife, that he was having this affair. The uninformed member of the marriage, the wife, found out about the affair after contracting HIV from her infected husband.

ASK DR. ANGELA® SERIES
ASK DR. ANGELA About Intimate and Other Partner Abuse and Violence

Entanglement itself is not necessarily intimacy.

Entanglement can masquerade as true intimacy and can also serve as the glue holding even a hollow or painful relationship together.

Take another look at intimacy: There is of course something — there has to be something — about the intimate partnership that tends to help distinguish it from other partnerships, such as the business partnership. YES, INTIMACY!

> **Intimacy.**
> **Intimacy.**
> **Intimacy, whatever that is.**

While this answer, intimacy, is of course obvious, it is still hauntingly ambiguous. How can something we can hardly understand and can barely identify be so powerful? Future, present, or past intimacy is one of the great, if not the greatest, influences upon a relationship. Yet, we still cannot entirely describe it, fully define its reaches and aspects.

Again and most certainly, when we say "intimacy" here, what comes to mind is usually "sexual" intimacy. Sexual intimacy must be interrogated for its actual effects on human relating. Could it be that this is the ingredient that separates one category of relationship from another, and should this be so? Does everything change once two people "have sex" together?

ASK DR. ANGELA
#701: Emotional and Physical Abuse in Relationships, Part One

INTIMACY AND MUTUAL BOUNDARY CROSSING

Sexual interaction does help explain acceptable boundary crossing (when that is what the sexual interaction is). Relationship intimacy contains a high degree of mutual boundary crossing WITH MUTUAL PERMISSION—such as what takes place during sex. Note again that if this supposed form of intimacy, sexual intimacy, takes place without mutual explicit permission, this is more like rape than interpersonal intimacy. There is nothing intimate about rape. Sexual assault is not intimate. Boundary crossing without permission hints at assault—hints and shouts assault.

The problem with looking for the clear cut division between sex with and sex without permission is that this matter is not always so clear cut, neither in casual nor in more serious relationships.

Best approach in terms of sexual intimacy is: where not sure the permission is clearly fully mutual, do not go there. However, this lack of clarity is too often settled for, and then boundaries are crossed without clear permission.

Participating in the sex act can be quite impulsive, as can surrendering to one's own or someone else's sex drive. Furthermore, "no" has many meanings including "absolutely not," and "maybe," "sorta'," " I guess so," "OK yes, yes," and "YES!"

Yes, we are back to consent. Although crossing the line into sexual relation carries a relationship into a certain zone—the sexually intimate zone—the decision to cross is not always a conscious one and is not always deliberate. In fact, some boundary crossings are not wanted but they are not stopped. Some boundary crossings are not wanted by even the *dominant boundary crosser*. And many boundary crossings are entirely misunderstood.

BOUNDARY CROSSING WITHOUT PERMISSION

Although this may seem to be returning to the most obvious, it must be said again and again. So, let's say it again: there is nothing, nothing, nothing intimate about boundary crossing without *clear* mutual permission. Without clear and true permission, THIS IS BOUNDARY RAPE, isn't it?

And yet, there are forms of and degrees of rape about which many people are confused. Here, sexual intimacy is being discussed because it is more readily seen as intimacy, whether or not it truly is. And then there are some crossings into sexual intimacy which a person wants and does not want at the same time.

This internal conflict is ignored or denied or even acknowledged and then trespassed upon anyway. Where a person consents to sex but does not want this sex, is this a raping of oneself then?

Impulse is fun and liberating, yet impulse can be a problem. So much sexual intimacy is engaged in on impulse. Parents of teenagers know this very well and tend to be very concerned about this. Quite wisely, parents often try to tell their teenagers to think before moving into sexual intimacy. Yet, how many times have these parents themselves given sex as little thought as they are concerned their offspring will?

ASK DR. ANGELA
#701: Emotional and Physical Abuse in Relationships, Part One

INTIMACY CAN OPEN DOORS

Intimacy takes a relationship to a new place. Intimacy can open doors to greater depth in relationship, and this can be one of the most positive experiences life has to offer. Deeply knowing and loving another human being is a precious experience, one worth seeking and protecting. Nothing said in this book denies the potential for great meaning and great beauty in intimate partner love.

At the same time, intimacy can open doors to places no one should have to go without understanding first what visiting these places can look like. Walk the intimacy path with respect and awareness, and with open eyes.

SEE THE DIFFERENCE BETWEEN PERMISSION TO CROSS AND VIOLATION OF BOUNDARIES

Do not travel into boundary crossing *without full and clear permission*. Here is where there is risk of rape (boundary crossing *without* permission), as well as of self abuse, relationship addiction, interpersonal abuse, and even violence. Here, in these difficult places, the interpersonal abuse and violence of boundary crossing itself can occur almost naturally, almost unnoticed at first. Or at least unacknowledged.

Clearly, *boundary crossing* is an ambiguous concept. The concept of *personal boundaries* is defined in various ways and is largely subjective. Most boundaries are themselves

ASK DR. ANGELA® SERIES
ASK DR. ANGELA About Intimate and Other Partner Abuse and Violence

ambiguous, and therefore of course very difficult to precisely define. Still, awareness of personal boundaries matters in interpersonal relating.

Much of *personal boundary awareness* is not only a matter of opinion and subjective, but also intuitive. Much of personal boundary awareness is vague, even subconscious. Yet, intimate partner relationships are traveling in or around the personal boundary territory most of the time.

Here, in this territory of the sub- and or un- conscious, there is at times rather careless and even dangerous relating. Some people find themselves walking a treacherous quicksand, a place where they can lose awareness of their own and others' boundaries, and of their lives. Here is where they can slip away from themselves and fall into problematic patterns of relating.

So, the sign on more than one door says "intimacy," but these doors open to very different places. Meet the brief or long term, casual or more serious, intimate partner here. Yes, maybe this potential or actual intimate partner is opening the door, and if so, hopefully is opening the door consciously, with great awareness of what is involved.

The partner wants to be clear minded, to love freely and at the same time to remain aware of her or his trades, agreements, and boundaries. Being aware even when in love helps know the possible and for some actual risk of problems that we are talking about in this book: troubled interpersonal issues, interactions, patterns, habits, even sometimes addictions, compulsions, abuses, and violences.

ASK DR. ANGELA
#701: Emotional and Physical Abuse in Relationships, Part One

RECOGNIZE VIO-LATION AS VIO-LENCE

Violence? Yes. Having one's boundary crossed *without permission* is having that boundary *violated*. To VIO-late a boundary is to do that boundary VIO-lence. VIO-lation of a partner's boundary IS ABUSE, IS VIOLENCE AGAINST THAT BOUNDARY.

ASK DR. ANGELA® SERIES
ASK DR. ANGELA About Intimate and Other Partner Abuse and Violence

ASK DR. ANGELA
#701: Emotional and Physical
Abuse in Relationships, Part One

Chapter 13
Anatomy of the Bond

Ultimately, we are looking for ourselves in our relationships as in all else we do. We seek ourselves through our relationships, involving, perhaps even using, other persons as counterparts, players in our searches. The "who am I" question constantly whispers to us. So, whether or not we catch ourselves doing this, we are constantly seeking mirrors, reflections of ourselves. What better mirror than a love relationship? After all, we might fool ourselves sweetly, implying that, "Who I am is who I am when I am with you." But do we hear ourselves when we may also be saying: "Without you, who am I? Much less? Nothing?"

LOVE CAN TRIGGER

Love relationships can serve as triggers for, identifiers of, interactions and bondings that help to bring out in us who we are, and who we are not. Our counterparts, whether or not we want them to or they want to, can trigger all kinds of things within us. Hobbies, interests, tastes, beliefs—also exercising, eating, spending, drinking, and other habits and behaviors—can be brought out in us via our interactions with someone we are close to or around a great deal.

And where particular interests and tendencies are not somewhere within us, we can sometimes take them on once in the ongoing close presence of someone who has those interests and tendencies. (Although not at all like the process

ASK DR. ANGELA® SERIES
ASK DR. ANGELA About Intimate and Other Partner Abuse and Violence

of a dog owner looking a little more like her or his dog over time, this is an interesting analogy.) *And, in itself, this becoming a bit like each other is not a problem. This can be an exciting and even deeply moving process. Meshing lives, perhaps even meshing selves to some extent, can be a highly rewarding process, a deepening of the self and soul.*

The challenge is to know whether we can take on tendencies, even some real behavioral characteristics, of another without hurting or losing ourselves or our own boundaries. With clear understanding of this process, we can manage to experience some degree of "losing ourselves in each other" (as it is often described) without getting lost. We can benefit by undergoing the bonding, meshing, intersection of lives and selves processes, with awareness. This can enable us to intersect with each other without losing our own boundaries.

Note: Where we lose too much of our own boundaries, we may do so to the point of weakening ourselves. Then we may reach a place of forgetting who we are as individuals and what we personally need and want. In this sense, we may commit a form of self abuse by being at this point. However, rarely do we consciously choose to do this to ourselves, and rarely do we choose to abuse ourselves like this.

In some troubled relationships, one partner is expected to be more and more the way the other partner expects her or him to be (whether this other partner wants to be these things): more attractive, more obedient, more compliant, more submissive in certain activities, more sexual on demand, and so on.

ASK DR. ANGELA
#701: Emotional and Physical Abuse in Relationships, Part One

BONDING AND TIME

Intense bonding, even in a very new love relationship, is natural. Love can be a beautiful bond, a deep emotional engagement and commitment, a truly rich experience making life all the more meaningful. Of course, entering into, and then existing as, an individual while in an intimate partner relationship is a never ending process. The relationship changes, just as its members do, as time goes by. The relationship develops a history of its own, a deeper meaning and identity of its own. The relationship can take on a personality of its own—not only in the eyes of outsiders who may even come to call the relationship the "Smiths" or the "couple next door" or "those two," but also in the eyes of its members.

When the members of the "couple" both feel that the evolution of their relationship is generally positive (appearing something like what is depicted in *Figure 13.1*), then the progression moves something like this although perhaps not precisely in this order:

- from initial attraction to deeper connection;
- to intersection of lives;
- to identification with the relationship;
- to formalization of the relationship;
- to perpetuation of the relationship;
- to preservation of the relationship;
- to ongoing deepening of the relationship and of the commitment to it.

SOME BONDS PROGRESS NEGATIVELY

Of course, there are other less than desirable paths a bond may take. It is important for persons in intimate partner relationships to track, or at least be aware of, the progression of their relationships, the evolution of their bonds, over time. The relationship and its members can maintain an awareness of the direction (or directions) their relationship is taking. They can even influence the direction, if paying close attention—relating consciously and recognizing signs such as those suggesting there may be a need for attention to, and work on, the relationship.

For example, a watchful eye early in a new relationship, when both love hormones and sexual passion can run very high, may help to prevent confusions, issues, and problem patterns from evolving early on in that relationship. Why ignore hints that a relationship might enter or take the path of a troubled or even problem progression?

(Such a progression can take many forms, including the one depicted in *Figure 13.2*. Note that the deterioration of a bond may take paths other than the one depicted in *Figure 13.2* and may fluctuate between periods of positive progression and periods of negative progression, as well as have reversals as suggested in *Figure 13.3*).

DO BONDS EVER BREAK OR END?

We hear talk of bonds being broken. However, what is frequently taking place is that the nature of the bond is changing and may or may not be deteriorating in quality. If

ASK DR. ANGELA
#701: Emotional and Physical Abuse in Relationships, Part One

the quality or strength of a relationship is in the process of weakening for some reason (not always a problem reason, sometimes just the result of time and change), there will eventually be a noticeable change in the bond between the partners in this relationship.

Bonds can continue long after a relationship "ends" or thinks it has ended. Of course, somewhere along the line, there may actually be no bond, the relationship may be entirely over, yet as long as there is something between the people in the relationship, no matter how distant they may grow, whether or not it feels good, there is a bond. There are even those who will argue that years after a couple has ended its relationship, even when there is no contact, a bond may continue to exist.

This is not necessarily a positive or comfortable bond, although it may be. It is simply some form of ongoing connection via family or memory, or other human "dots" which remain connected to each.

ILLUSIONS

Bonds (or what those bonds once were if they ever were this) can continue to appear to exist when these bonds no longer exist. And, also, bonds (or what those bonds once were if they ever were this) can appear not to exist (any longer) when these bonds nevertheless continue to exist.

To some degree, we are always dealing with some degree of illusion when seeing bonds have been formed, maintained, and or ended. Frequent and highly conscious reality checks are essential at all points in relationships, even in life.

Figure 13.1.
Anatomy of a probable positive bond progression.

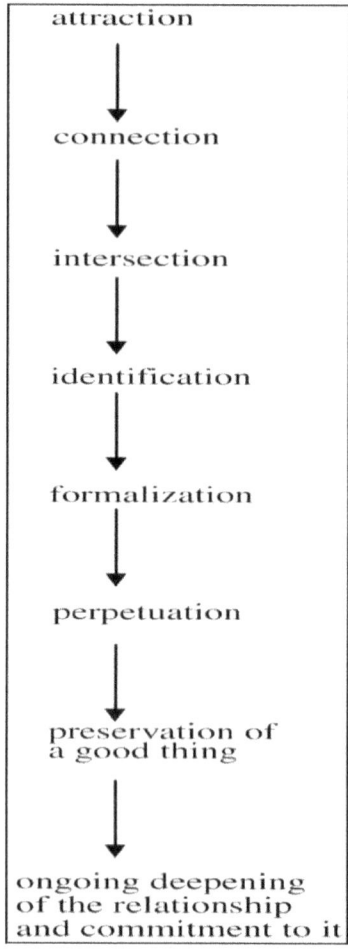

**Figure 13.2.
Anatomy of a probable negative bond progression.**

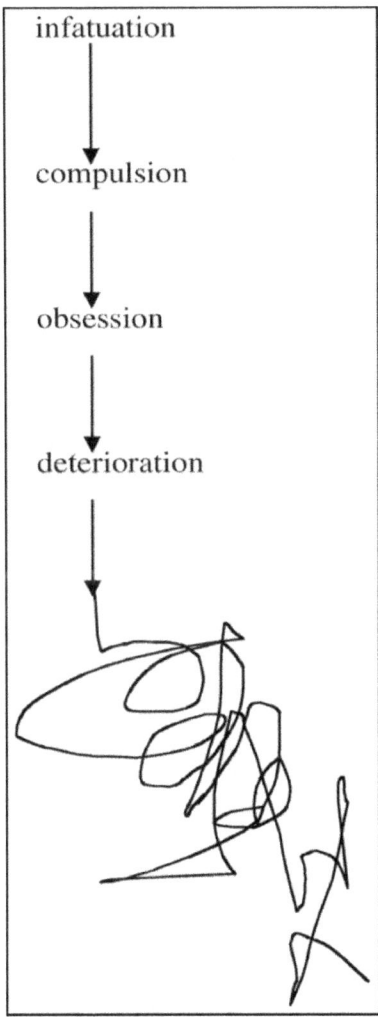

ASK DR. ANGELA® SERIES
ASK DR. ANGELA About Intimate and Other Partner Abuse and Violence

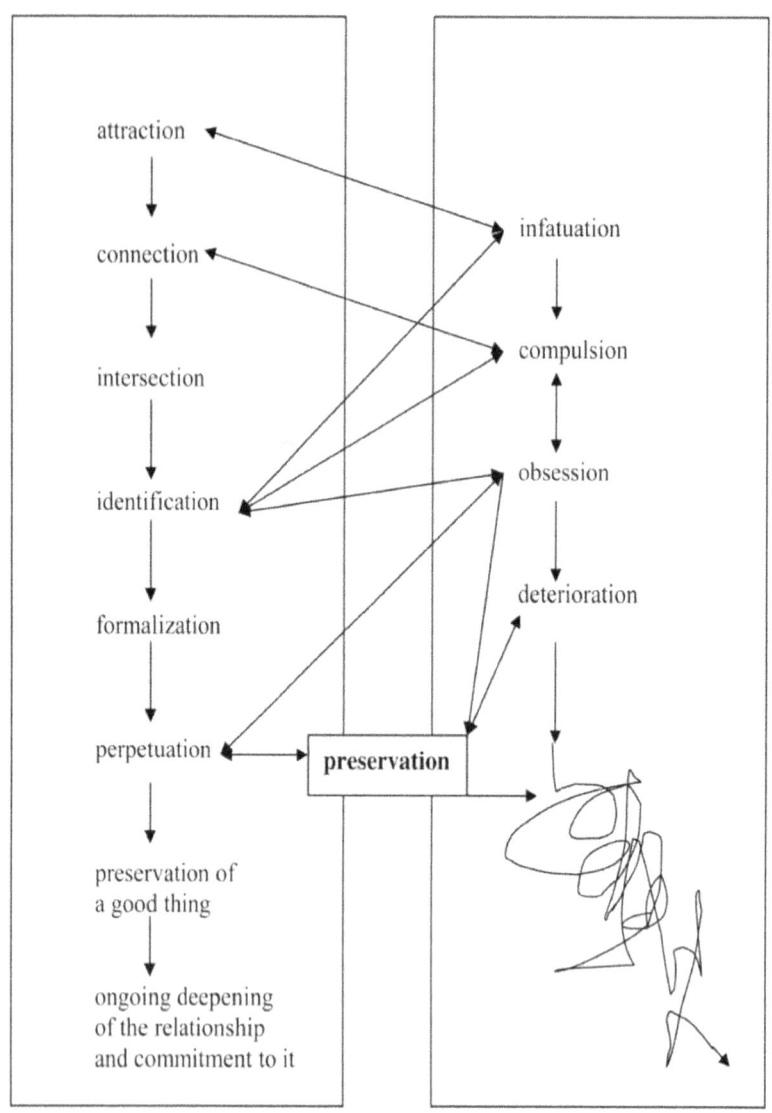

Figure 13.3.
Example of a mixed positive and negative bond progression with reversals.

ASK DR. ANGELA
#701: Emotional and Physical
Abuse in Relationships, Part One

Chapter 14
Messages Story

There was an eleven month separation leading up to their divorce. About one-third of the way through this separation, Beth was completely uncertain as to what Stewart's true intentions were. She was broke, unable to pay bills that Stewart and she had long ago put in her name. She felt financially stranded.

Stewart was the one who had filed for divorce, yet he continued to communicate to her that he was very sorry he had done so and that he did not really want a divorce. He begged Beth for forgiveness many times. Beth was either fooled or confused, or both, and this state of mind continued to plague her for the duration of the separation.

Halfway through the pre-divorce separation, Stewart had his attorney send a letter stating that Stewart had "renewed his commitment to reconciliation," and that he assumed that Beth was "in agreement on this." The letter also stated that Stewart had been committed to reconciliation since the start of the separation. Beth was quite confused by this.

Throughout the separation there was mixed communication coming from Stewart regarding their dividing their property without a divorce.

One moment, Stewart wanted to "forget everything and go back to the way things were," and the next, he wanted to "legally sever the property and then stay married."

ASK DR. ANGELA® SERIES
ASK DR. ANGELA About Intimate and Other Partner Abuse and Violence

And the next moment he wanted out no matter what this meant.

The pressure to sever the property increased as the months went by, but Stewart still wavered on even this matter. Beth really could not make sense out of what Stewart was telling her, and found the idea that they would stay married while severing their finances odd as they had shared everything for so long. As the months wore on, Beth grew very tired, felt that the confusion was not going to end, and that, now that all this had taken place, she could never feel quite the same about Stewart.

Against the backdrop of ongoing emotional pleas made by Stewart to Beth to never leave him, Stewart made concurrent threatening demands (including threats of violence against her and even of killing her) that she agree to whatever financial demands he was making.

Beth found herself increasingly sick, fearful, and wanting to get as far away from Stewart as she could. As she grew more definite about wanting the divorce, Stewart grew angrier that she was.

ASK DR. ANGELA
#701: Emotional and Physical
Abuse in Relationships, Part One

Chapter 15
Signs

After two decades of being married, and living and sleeping together, a few of you might wake up one morning and find a stranger in your bed—your spouse! How well do we really know the people we sleep with, love, and spend the time of our lives with? Any better than we know ourselves?

When the person with whom you've been emotionally and physically intimate for so many years becomes a stranger to you, is this strangeness retroactive—does this mean that this person was a stranger to you all along without your knowing this?

If so, were you fooled into thinking you ever knew this person? Or were you fooling yourself? Do you know? *Were you having intercourse with a stranger when you thought this person was your significant other? Who was fooling whom? Who betrayed whom? Anyone? Anyone at all?*

Who (either knowingly or unknowingly) stepped over the line, masquerading as a known person, as a recognized intimate partner, hiding behind the mask of familiarity and love while secretly remaining a stranger—or eventually becoming one? Or is this just (and most likely) you both simply moving through your lives and now having new parts of yourselves to share with each other? ... Or to not share with each other?

ASK DR. ANGELA® SERIES
ASK DR. ANGELA About Intimate and Other Partner Abuse and Violence

SLIPPING INTO BOUNDARY CONFUSION

We might see this as being about boundaries—whose boundaries these are, where these boundaries are, whether these boundaries are anywhere, how clear these boundaries are—and whether these boundaries are wanted.

All relationships are at risk of boundary confusions, boundary crossings, whether due to personal change, unbridled enthusiasm, mistakes, carelessness, lies, betrayals, or other positive and less than positive conditions such as problem patterns, habits, and addictions.

Many partners process these events well, carefully, and grow from these. Boundaries can mature. Partners can grow to further define and respect their own and their partner's and their relationship's boundaries. Even when these all do appear to be the same boundaries, these are not, as the self, the partner, and the relationship are three (at least three) different systems.

However, too many relationships unknowingly slip into patterns of boundary confusions, boundary crossings, and boundary betrayals, and the behaviors which accompany these, the latter of which can be boundary abuses.

This is not just a matter of an occasional, "Hey wait, that's my toothbrush, use yours," or, "You used all the clean towels in one hour." This is more a matter of one partner stepping over the line into the other partner's personal domain, personal territory—or maybe even outside boundaries beyond the

ASK DR. ANGELA
#701: Emotional and Physical Abuse in Relationships, Part One

relationship's own sexual, emotional, financial, or other boundaries.

This can also be the failure of the relationship to continuously and mutually redefine itself as the relationship moves through life — redefine itself both to its members and to the world.

When the relationship's boundaries are not well or clearly defined, then the boundaries can be crossed (purposefully, or carelessly, or mistakenly) by those within and around the relationship. This can result in extra-marital or extra-relationship affairs taking place without both of the partners clearly knowing and consenting, and or financial deceptions where shared monies are hidden or relabeled or pilfered without one of the partners knowing the other is so doing, and or other *boundary transgressions.*

(Note that this is not a judgment on the practice of extra-marital affairs. Rather this is a clear statement regarding relationship boundaries and how these are only effective *and real* when *both* partners are clear on these and respect these. Where *both* partners are not clear on the same boundaries, there is actually no shared or respected boundary.)

Again, we come to this matter of boundary crossing without permission. How can it be that so many do not see the problem — boundary crossing becoming boundary abuse — approaching and or getting worse? Sometimes we just do not want to see, and other times, we simply do not know how to look — or what to look for.

ASK DR. ANGELA® SERIES
ASK DR. ANGELA About Intimate and Other Partner Abuse and Violence

WATCHING FOR SIGNS OF BOUNDARY ABUSE

Then there is the matter of purposeful boundary betrayal, also a boundary crossing, a more complicated version. This is a partner's knowing breaking of an implied or actual agreement to define, respect, and stick to boundaries which define—form, protect—the relationship. A popular example is secret, undisclosed, infidelity which takes place when an agreed upon, promised, boundary—such as not to be sexually intimate with anyone else—is broken.

> **Respecting the relationship's boundaries means not crossing these boundaries unless *both* partners clearly explicitly consent in advance of the crossing.**

If the basic agreement of the relationship and its own boundaries requires revision, this is best done consciously, directly, no matter how difficult. Honestly rather than secretly treading across boundaries avoids *boundary abuse, and the partner abuse this includes.*

Again note that sexual infidelity can be a ready example of treading over mutually agreed upon boundaries, but in many ways, one of the easier to define. Emotional infidelity—taking the emotional intimacy of the intimate partnership elsewhere—can also be betrayal.

Some people weigh sexual infidelity as more serious than emotional infidelity, while others say the opposite. *Decisions to cross sexual, emotional, and other relationship boundaries should*

ASK DR. ANGELA
#701: Emotional and Physical Abuse in Relationships, Part One

be those of the partners in the relationship, and these are decisions that should be made by them up front and together.

Clarifying all this, and keeping partners clear about it, involves having basic and clear founding and ongoing agreements between the partners as they grow and change. Ideally these are explicit, maybe even written agreements, so both partners can take the *founding agreements* seriously—or know when these are no longer in place.

This is not to judge fidelity and or infidelity here, rather this is to say that both partners have a right to know what the agreement regarding all this is, and if this agreement is still in place or has been broken.

Unfortunately, many relationships are formed without very clear, very explicit, very specific agreements about many things such as fidelity. Implicit agreements such as, "Well, I thought that is what we meant when we got together, but we never really made it clear, I guess" are not sufficient in many cases.

Betrayal and infidelity are only some of the boundary abuses that can take place in unclear, vague, confused, and troubled relationships. Almost more difficult are the harder to label boundary abuses.

So pay attention. *Love does not have to be blind. There is nothing wrong with falling in love with one's eyes wide open.* Staying alert and watching for signs of possibly emerging boundary confusion and abuse is not a bad thing to be doing. Partners can do this together, consciously, intelligently.

ASK DR. ANGELA® SERIES
ASK DR. ANGELA About Intimate and Other Partner Abuse and Violence

And, watching for signs does not have to be hard work....

Watching for signs does require honesty with each other—but first and foremost honesty with oneself! A great deal of focus falls on the problem of members of relationships not being honest with each other, and much less on each of the members not being honest with themselves.

It's pretty much a hot seat, a don't-touch topic: Do we know what it feels like to be honest with ourselves? Can we ask someone else to be honest with us if we are not honest with ourselves? Yes, surely we can. *We have a right to demand honesty in a relationship.*

Still, when we are deceiving, or lying, to ourselves about the relationship—or simply looking away from abuse dangers being experienced--we are at risk of betraying ourselves. Best to demand truth of ourselves as well as of our partners. If we are in danger, it is best to let ourselves know this.

Note: Too frequently, persons being even physically abused, even beaten, deny to themselves and to concerned outsiders that this abuse is taking place. This denial itself can be quite dangerous. Unfortunately, the alternative to this denial, truth itself, or demanding truth itself, can also be dangerous.

What are the signs that a relationship is a troubled or problem relationship? A combination of indicators coming from within and from around ourselves tells us what we need to know, if we are paying attention.

This chapter discusses indicators coming from within. Basically, indicators coming from within are indicators that

ASK DR. ANGELA
#701: Emotional and Physical Abuse in Relationships, Part One

the person feeling these things is not comfortable—with something.

Figure 15.1 suggests some key indicators and a method of rating these indicators in terms of their significance to us. Let's think of these indicators in terms of their value as signs that we may not be entirely comfortable—And, in this case, we may not be comfortable in a particular intimate partner relationship, or in some aspect of that relationship.

Keep in mind that *Figure 15.1* rates the individual's comfort level and not the quality of the relationship. However, if one or both members are very uncomfortable in these ways, then there is something, some corner of the heart or soul, asking for attention. The following pages discuss the factors listed in *Figure 15.1*.

VAGUE FREE-FLOATING DISCOMFORT

Everyone has experienced at some point a vague feeling of discomfort, a feeling that something is just not right, something but not anything specific. *This is ourselves sending ourselves a notice. The letters may be faint and hard to read, but the handwriting is on the wall.*

Unexplainable exhaustion, sadness, edginess, confusion, and even more extreme sensations such as nausea, headaches, and body aches—these can be signs from the self to the self.

These can be signals saying, "Hey, wake up, there could be a problem here." Of course, if there is a problem, it could be stemming from any number of things, including of course physical health issues, and not necessarily from a relationship. Or these could be signs of minor issues that quickly fade away.

Still these symptoms are indeed messages from the self to the self revealing that something is going on. *(If these signs do continue, see a medical doctor to test for health issues. However, where tests show no medical issues, then ask whether perhaps these messages are coming from you to yourself for another reason.)*

The signs do not have to be entirely negative. Within reason, a sign such as increased dedication to one's work or perhaps to one's exercise program can be a good thing. Yet, these might for some reason also be an avoidance of, or escape from facing, reality. When the reality is trouble in an intimate partner relationship, we are not always ready to see this. We may even work to avoid this, to cover it up, to be too busy to see it, to arrange with ourselves to simply not see it. *Not-seeing: this is denial.*

The thing about our subconscious minds not allowing our conscious minds to see what is going on right before our very eyes is that the messages we are suppressing crop up everywhere anyway. We start to know that something is just not right. Something, yes, but not necessarily anything specific....

...Vague, free-floating feelings of discomfort wander, or even flood, in.

NOT FEELING LIKE ONESELF

Another subtle sign is the sense of not feeling like oneself.

ASK DR. ANGELA
#701: Emotional and Physical Abuse in Relationships, Part One

"I'm just not myself these days." "Sometimes I wonder what drives me." "I don't know how I feel about that or about anything right now." Also in this not feeling like oneself category is the *sense of inauthenticity*. "Nothing about what I am saying sounds like me." "I don't really know who I am anymore."

We truly can have times when we truly do not know how we feel. Or we can subconsciously choose not to realize we feel inauthentic. We can lie to ourselves and not realize we are doing so; we can lie to ourselves and fool ourselves into thinking we are not lying. There are so many subtle ways to avoid the truth about something, very likely the truth about our feelings.

CHOOSING TO AVOID THE TRUTH

And, certainly there are times when one consciously chooses to avoid the truth, making a clear and conscious decision to do so.

Why not, we tell ourselves: "The world is full of lies, it runs on lies for the most part, why not my intimate partner relationship too," and, "Too much truth is like taking a medicine which is too strong: it can make you sick," and, "Little lies, well, they save us unnecessary pain."

> **Choosing to avoid the truth**
> **is all too common.**
>
> **In fact, for many,**
> **this is a way of life.**

ASK DR. ANGELA® SERIES
ASK DR. ANGELA About Intimate and Other Partner Abuse and Violence

SENSE OF PLAYING A ROLE

What consciously or subconsciously avoiding truth, *or even actually living with lies*, does is create a *hideout from reality*. Wherever truth might shake things up and bring about unforeseen changes, the fear of change may hold back the truth. *Yes, some truths are explosive if and when told. The alternative then, in many minds, is never to tell them.* Similarly, many people prefer to be lied to and even tell their partners, "Of course I don't want you to, but don't tell me about it if you go to bed with someone else," and, "Some things are better left unsaid."

This sort of warding off of the truth casts the real life one is leading into a sort of stage set atmosphere. Everything is an act, because everything must avoid the truth which is not being told. Everything is quite scripted, even if done subconsciously. Everything is designed to speak around what is not being said. *Out of this comes a sense, sometimes a deeply buried sense but nevertheless a sense, that one is playing a role rather than being entirely real.*

HOLLOW OR UNFULFILLING INTIMACY

All of the above effects are some key elements of discomfort—with something. These signs can be telling us to pay attention—to something. And, this can be to ourselves, to our relationships, or to something else. The same is true for intimacy issues. These can be signs of many different things and not only that there is a problem with an intimate partner relationship.

ASK DR. ANGELA
#701: Emotional and Physical Abuse in Relationships, Part One

Hollow and or unfulfilling physical, sexual, emotional, and or other intimacy (whatever of these intimacies are part of a particular relationship's life) may well be an indication that something is not quite right. Experiencing these, we may be sensing something about ourselves or about our partners and not realize that we are doing so. For example, engaging in sexual intimacy when not wanting to do so, or not wanting to do so very much, or not enjoying it, is a sign that a person is doing something a least a bit alien to her or his best interests at that time.

Recall the earlier discussion of rape being crossing boundaries without permission. Here, this person "willingly" engaging in sex without wanting it, or while feeling that something is not quite right, is in a sense allowing her or his boundaries to be crossed without her or his own permission.

This is almost a self betrayal, or yes, on some level, almost a self rape sort of event. Being willing to do this to oneself is a sign that something is awry. This calls for some deep introspection:

What value do we place on our own personal boundaries, on ourselves, and on our relationships when we "allow" this sort of thing to take place? What does "allow" actually mean here?

Whether this sense of hollow intimacy comes on this profoundly, or simply takes the form of a lingering but vague feeling of hollowness during intimate interactions, there is a message from self to self in the experience. Anything which we continue to engage in after it becomes hollow and unfulfilling deserves at least some of our attention. Why are we doing this while feeling this way? Do we feel good about doing this while feeling this way?

Might this hollow, unfulfilled, self-betrayed feeling be a sign that we need to stop and look deeply in order to acknowledge that some kind of disconnect is taking place?

FEELING LIKE SOMETHING IS WRONG

Reaching far beyond free floating discomfort, this nagging, haunting sense that something is wrong, perhaps very wrong, works its way into our consciousness quite slowly, creeping in from the vague subconscious realm. This sensation may be with us for quite some time before we recognize it. Or, it may be with us for quite some time while we choose to ignore or deny its presence. Sometimes we just do not want to know that something is wrong, as once we know this consciously, we may call upon ourselves to actually do something about it.

And frequently, the sense that something is wrong is not attached to anything specific.

Yes, this could be denial at work, or it could be that we are not fully understanding what this discomfort or "wrong thing" or "wrongness" might be. Nevertheless, this sensation must be respected and given attention. Stop and feel. That's all it takes. Stop and feel that something is going on, and that that something may be confusing, uncomfortable, or wrong—or not, and that that something may be something which cannot be labeled as of yet.

ASK DR. ANGELA
#701: Emotional and Physical Abuse in Relationships, Part One

FEELING TRAPPED

And then there is the sensation of feeling trapped. This can register with us as stagnation, confusion, depression, frustration, tension, claustrophobia, anger, or other troubled emotions.

An animal in a maze with no exit does not know what the maze is, does not know why he or she was placed there, and does not imagine that perhaps he or she created this maze or at least willingly entered it. But, eventually the animal does come to feel trapped and does demonstrate this in any number of ways including being lazy, or frantic, or aggressive toward itself or others.

The looming sense of being trapped must be listened to. A prolonged trapped sense, a lasting "no exit" sensation, is not healthy and, if unaddressed for too long, can lead to problematic mental and physical conditions, and even abrupt unexpected outbursts of depression, anger, rage, and or violence.

If you feel trapped, pay attention to the feeling. Feel it, and feel it more. Find safe places and friends with which to share what is going on. When understood, frequently with professional guidance, this sensation can be worked with and moved beyond.[6]

---

[6] For an example of guided and therapeutic release from this trapped no exit sensation, see the book where I detail this matter, *SEEING THE HIDDEN FACE OF ADDICTION*.

ASK DR. ANGELA® SERIES
ASK DR. ANGELA About Intimate and Other Partner Abuse and Violence

DENYING SIGNS

How often do we ignore these signs, especially the early warning signs, in hopes that things will simply get better? How much of this ignoring, which often continues on while a relationship does NOT get better, is part of the larger problem of denial?

A person living with or in a troubled relationship, or who is feeling troubled about that relationship, if paying attention, can note many signs that there is something to be looking at.

When there is something to be known, the signs are all around, yet quite frequently hard to see or not seen. Denial again. It's that same old denial! Denial serves its purpose—it denies the existence or reality it seeks to deny. Meanwhile, vague free floating feelings of unlabeled discomfort and agitation follow us around, nag us, until we turn and face these.

A troubled relationship is usually troubled long before the trouble is addressed or even recognized.

ASK DR. ANGELA
#701: Emotional and Physical Abuse in Relationships, Part One

SIGNS WHICH MAY BE TELLING US WE ARE TROUBLED BY OUR INTIMATE PARTNER RELATIONSHIP:
MEASUREMENTS
directions for use:

1. There are several scales listed here in Figure 15.1.

1. Vague Free-Floating Discomfort

free-floating discomfort scale
1--------------------5--------------------10
no or little   maximum

2. Not Feeling Like Oneself

not feeling like oneself scale
1--------------------5--------------------10
no or little   maximum

3. Choosing to Avoid the Truth

choosing to avoid the truth scale
1--------------------5--------------------10
no or little   maximum

4. Sense of Playing a Role

sense of playing a role scale
1--------------------5--------------------10
no or little   maximum

5. Hollow or Unfulfilling Intimacy

hollow or unfulfilling intimacy scale
1--------------------5--------------------10
no or little   maximum

6. Feeling Like Something is Wrong

feeling like something is wrong scale
1--------------------5--------------------10
no or little   maximum

7. Feeling Trapped

Feeling trapped scale
1--------------------5--------------------10
no or little   maximum

2. Design or add other scales which you feel provide you other signs that you may indeed be in a troubled relationship or at least feel that you are.

3. Give your experience in each area for which there is a scale listed a number – a place on the scale. This number will be from 1 to 10 with 1 being a low level of experience in this area and 10 being the highest level of experience in this area.

4. If you are not feeling anything in the area of a particular scale, give yourself no number or rating, which means this will be a zero for you.

5. Add the numbers for the scales together. A person who is a five on each of these scales will have a total of 35 (7 x 5) if the questions on the left are used.

6. Now compute the average of the responses you gave yourself for each scale on which you scored yourself other than zero: If the chart on the left is used as is, then your total will be divided by 7. If your total was 35, then compute 35 divided by 7=5.

7. Your average would therefore be 5.

8. Any average of 5 or higher *may* indicate that there are signs that you are either troubled by your relationship or you are in a troubled relationship. Even an average response of 3 suggests that something is calling your attention. Whether or not it be your feelings about your relationship, you are telling yourself something.

Figure 15.1. Signs which may be telling us we are troubled by our intimate partner relationship.

ASK DR. ANGELA® SERIES
ASK DR. ANGELA About Intimate and Other Partner Abuse and Violence

ASK DR. ANGELA
#701: Emotional and Physical
Abuse in Relationships, Part One

Chapter 16
Any Idea Story

Chris and Jan were together over ten years before one of them, Chris, quite suddenly decided to leave the relationship.

This came as a complete surprise to Jan, who had had no idea that there was a problem. They had come together in the early stages of two up-swinging careers, had had no problems or disagreements along the way, and found living together not only convenient but a good idea. They liked the same foods, the same colors, and the same music, and they kept the same hours. Very early on, they decided they were extremely compatible and that was that.

What Jan had not realized was that Chris was not entirely happy with the arrangement, because Chris did not really like health food that much, longed for red meat which they did not eat, hated the persimmon color they painted their walls, definitely hated classical music, and really needed much more sleep.

That Jan had not realized this was surprising, but not as surprising as the fact that Chris had not consciously realized any of this either, not until the moment the entire relationship ended. From one moment to the next, the denial fizzled and reality set in. At least for Chris it did.

While this was powerfully freeing for Chris, this was debilitating and demoralizing for Jan who felt that the investment of over a decade of time in this relationship had virtually been what Jan now decided to call a "complete lie."

**ASK DR. ANGELA® SERIES
ASK DR. ANGELA About Intimate and Other Partner
Abuse and Violence**

And while this accusation made Chris very angry, Chris knew that this was actually true, that Chris had been lying all along. However, Chris had been deceiving Chris at least as much as Chris had been deceiving Jan.

ASK DR. ANGELA
#701: Emotional and Physical
Abuse in Relationships, Part One

Chapter 17
Denial?

Denial is a dangerous drug. Denial is an illusion supported by those in denial and quite often also by those around them. Denial is a way of seeing something other than what we truly see before us. Or better stated, denial is a way of thinking we are not-seeing what is right there before us, and instead seeing what we choose to see.

WE HAVE THE TENDENCY TO NOT SEE

If this book were restricted to but one message (a message which is indeed repeated in various forms several times herein), this would be it:

We have this tendency to not see what is going on around us when we do not want to know about it. And this tendency can be damaging and dangerous.

But first, an important note: Yes, we can fool or lie to ourselves. And we can also be fooled by others and be lied to by others. There is no denying this.

We are not guilty of telling the lies which others have told us when we thought they were telling us the truth. We cannot be expected to detect and decipher each and every lie we are told, every hidden truth behind each lie, and every detail about that truth.

ASK DR. ANGELA® SERIES
ASK DR. ANGELA About Intimate and Other Partner Abuse and Violence

How can we possibly filter everything coming at us from outside ourselves? (Or maybe even from inside?)

Yes, of course we can also be lied to by people other than ourselves. And, we can simply not realize or not see this. Yet, while this is going on, we can nevertheless feel on some level, in some way, there is some sort of problem.

We may not be able to give ourselves a detailed description of this problem, however we may have a general sense that there is something off, unclear, or maybe wrong.

However, all too often, the person sensing this something, if attempting to ask the partner about it, is shut down, ridiculed, and sometimes even beaten verbally or physically just for asking, for so-called "doubting."

As a result, the person simply feels that something, something not easy to pinpoint, but something, is terribly askew. This nagging feeling is often ignored, suppressed, denied, and sometimes even denied out of fear of danger. In actual, and or potentially, physically violent relationships, the risk of this denial (denial of danger or possible danger) is definitely a physical risk and can include injury, even serious injury or death.

This process of what this book defines as a
<u>not-seeing</u>
is a looking away from reality.

When an intimate partner relationship is entangled in a web of deception, the relationship is for the most part not with the

ASK DR. ANGELA
#701: Emotional and Physical Abuse in Relationships, Part One

other person but with the web of deception that has been built.

So now, is the relationship shifting to that between the individual and the web of deception itself? Who is the enforcer of this relationship? Who allows this web of deception to dominate the relationship? Isn't insisting that deception must not be called out, and must not be questioned, abuse in itself?

*(What, I'm not involved with you? I'm involved with what I tell myself is who you are, with what I tell myself is going on here? Or maybe I'm involved with the person **you** tell me **you** are, not you. Or maybe this **is** who are truly are.)*

DENIAL SNEAKS IN

So, denial has many faces and masks itself in many ways. At first, denial sneaks in, largely unseen, or under some other label such as: co-operating, being considerate, adapting, compromising, going along with things, doing what is best, giving in, doing what works—whatever works. Let's be clear: none of these things is so bad in the form of a single incident, even as a string of incidents, and many of these things can be components of a relationship that works rather well.

Problematic denial creeps in when we take steps down a path where we get lost, get damaged, die inside, die in some way—and where the denial process blocks awareness of emotional and physical safety.

In troubled relationships, problem denial, even dangerous denial, can find its way in through every crack in the wall, every chink in the *armor of the relationship*. Denial creeps in and wants to stay in. Denial itself becomes the glue holding things together. The composite, the whole picture, is then …

a facade not a relationship—
a false front—an act covering over a lack of awareness…
buttressed by denial upon denial …
facilitating the not-seeing of
the steps toward participating in, allowing…
anything needed to preserve the relationship.

Again, this relationship by now is not really between two people, but between their separate perceptions of themselves in the face of what they think is taking place. Frequently, this transition into denial is relatively innocuous. (See Figure 17.1 here below.)

> cooperating/ being considerate
> adapting / compromising
> **going along with things / doing what is best/ giving in**
> doing what works – whatever works
> doing what works – whatever works
> doing what works – whatever works
> doing what works – whatever works
> doing what works – whatever works
> doing what works – whatever works
> absolutely whatever works

Figure 17.1. Whatever works.

ASK DR. ANGELA
#701: Emotional and Physical
Abuse in Relationships, Part One

Chapter 18
What Strength Story

She had carefully prepared yet another gourmet dinner. Now she was about to put the plates in the oven to warm them to the perfect temperature so that the meal could be served on perfectly warm but not hot plates.

He had just then arrived home.

Immediately, for no clear reason, they were in the midst of yet one more angry and loud discussion about something minor. The debate went on for several minutes, and then, as was his usual behavior, he suddenly turned and walked out.

She waited a while, in fact for three hours, for his return, trying to keep the meal warm but not let it dry out, as she had done so many times before.

Tonight was different, she felt different, although she could not say why. Hungry, she finally ate her share of the meal and put his in the garbage.

An hour after that, he returned home and looked for his dinner. Finally he asked her where she had put it.

She told him she threw it away.

Upset and shocked, he tried to put some dinner together for himself, pulling what he could out of the garbage, slamming refrigerator and cabinet doors, and calling his mother long distance on the kitchen speaker phone as he did. When his mother came on the line, he complained about how his wife had thrown his dinner into the garbage just because he was a few hours late.

The speaker phone crackled with a long distance sigh as his mother replied:

"WHAT STRENGTH. I SHOULD HAVE DONE THAT TO YOUR FATHER YEARS AGO."

ASK DR. ANGELA
#701: Emotional and Physical
Abuse in Relationships, Part One

Chapter 19
Emotional Abuse Itself, And Emotional Abuse Against The Backdrop Of Threatened Or Actual Physical Abuse

Now you see it, now you don't. So tangled and murky it defies us to sort it out is the elusive matter of emotional abuse. After all, actual physical abuse can be difficult enough for some to detect and identify. Emotional abuse leaves vague traces of itself, many twisted tracks leading in different directions all at once. Questions about when this abuse is serious, what of it is damaging, who causes it, who feels it, and what the reason for it is are painful, disturbing, and challenging.

AGAINST THE BACKDROP OF
THREATENED AND ACTUAL PHYSICAL ABUSE

Any discussion of emotional abuse must note that many persons being emotionally abused are actually experiencing pressure to accept, endure, not stand up to, this emotional abuse. Threats of physical violence, and or actual physical violence, are frequently made to force the abusEE to simply accept the emotional abuse. The running undercurrent of this physical threat is what I define as *EMOTIONAL EXTORTION*. (Also note, other levels of extortion can be taking place at the same time, such as what I, in later books in this series, define as *EMOTIONAL AND PHYSICAL*

ASK DR. ANGELA® SERIES
ASK DR. ANGELA About Intimate and Other Partner Abuse and Violence

FINANCIAL EXTORTION. Cases where persons being abused lose access to their assets, even lose control of their assets, under pressure coming from the person abusing, are all too frequent.)

The following elements of emotional abuse may appear where there is no physical violence, and may appear where there is physical violence or the threat of this violence. Later books in this series continue this discussion.

TANGLED AND MURKY TYPE OF ABUSE

Emotional abuse is taking place all around us, and affects almost every one of us at least in a minor form at some time in our lives. Emotional abuse is so very common that we practically take it for granted, as normal and acceptable.

Emotional abuse tends to take a back seat to concerns about physical abuse as physical abuse is seen, at least by law enforcement and the courts, as more damaging, more dangerous, and more specific. And indeed, physical abuse is frequently an assault or attack or rape or other physical crime. And indeed, physical abuse is generally more dangerous and more identifiable, more specific. Therefore physical abuse is and must be the more readily addressed, and more a definable abuse.

This is not to downplay the significance and perceived seriousness of emotional abuse. Nevertheless, emotional abuse is frequently downplayed, even denied.

ASK DR. ANGELA
#701: Emotional and Physical Abuse in Relationships, Part One

In fact, many persons who are being abused emotionally but not physically do not recognize this abuse as there appear to be no physical signs of it. And of those being abused physically, many do not include emotional abuse in their descriptions of the abuse they are experiencing. However, the effects of some emotional abuse can be just as powerful as the effects of some physical abuse.

A note of reminder here. The discussion in this book deals with emotional (and physical) abuse *of adults by adults*. When children experience abuse, and far too many do, a host of highly critical factors not addressed in this book are present and require specific attention. Here, the discussion focuses on what is behavior taking place between two adults in a love, marital, dating, and or sexual relationship. *(This book can also apply to persons near adult age, teens, as in too many instances teens in relationships can also experience many of the IPV issues discussed in this book. Refer to the Author's Note at the opening of this book.)*

SIGNS OF EMOTIONAL ABUSE

Even adults experiencing emotional abuse may not see that this abuse is taking place. They may experience general indicators that something is awry (such as those indicators listed in Chapter 14). Again, those general indicators or signs may or may not be related to being the victim of emotional abuse. Yet, it is important to know that emotional abuse can cause, bring out, or magnify where already present, general indicators or signs of general discomfort or distress.

ASK DR. ANGELA® SERIES
ASK DR. ANGELA About Intimate and Other Partner Abuse and Violence

Beyond the general feelings of discomfort listed in *Chapter 15*, people who are actually experiencing emotional abuse may also experience more specific feelings of discomfort such as these listed here below. These signs may or may not be caused by, or attributed to, emotional abuse (not even in instances of high levels of emotional abuse), however these are quite common responses to emotional abuse in intimate partner relationships:

- Embarrassment.
- Confusion.
- Instability.
- Fear.
- Identity doubts, not feeling like oneself.
- Worthlessness, low self esteem.
- No or low level of confidence.
- Sense of complete or extreme failure.
- Depression.
- Isolation.
- No sense of control over what happens.
- All encompassing self blame—for every problem.
- Humiliation.
- Pessimism, a negative outlook on the future.

And eventually, persons being emotionally (including but not limited to verbally) abused by a partner over long periods of time may add to this list:

- Feeling that the criticisms of oneself being made by an abusive partner are correct, actually believing these.

ASK DR. ANGELA
#701: Emotional and Physical Abuse in Relationships, Part One

And even...

- Defending these criticisms to others.

And sadly, sometimes these self abusing behaviors also arise:

- Joining in on the emotional abuse of oneself.
- Amplifying the abuse being experienced by working to hurt oneself even more than the abuser does.
- Allowing, even inviting, physical and sexual abuse of oneself to take place unprotested or weakly protested.
- Hiding the pain of the abuse in substance abuse or other detrimental habitual behavior.
- Bottling up of rage.
- Hurting oneself emotionally or physically.
- Showing tendencies of suicidality.

And of course, what deserves entire volumes and is reported in depth elsewhere, is the risk that the abuse being experienced is then transferred onto others such as children. (See *Chapter 3* of this book, especially the sections there on *Collateral Abuse*. See also the next two books in this series, *ASK DR. ANGELA #702 and #703*.)

HARD TO SEE AND INVISIBLE ABUSE

Countless other feelings and attitudes can be found in persons experiencing emotional abuse. However, what is taking place during emotional abuse is in large part invisible as the abuse is occurring not only explicitly, such as audibly (verbally) and visibly, but also quietly, invisibly, and often

ASK DR. ANGELA® SERIES
ASK DR. ANGELA About Intimate and Other Partner Abuse and Violence

quite implicitly, even in many cases secretly.

It is perhaps the implicit, invisible abuse that is most difficult for the person being abused to deal with, as there is little if any validation that it is taking place. Other people (for the most part) do not see it, so they do not acknowledge it is happening, and in fact, they may if asked deny this is happening.

This can be a confusing, disturbing, even so-called crazy-making experience in that the person being abused is not only suffering the abuse but also feels that there is no reality to the experience—a potentially dangerous combination for one's mental and physical health.

(Note: While this is similar to self or others' denial, this may indeed be something else such as: lack of knowledge regarding abuse and violence; particular denial-like childhood experiences with, and messages from, parents; lack of self-awareness; poor self-confidence; self-destructive tendencies; etc.)

INVALIDATING

Abusers administering emotional abuse tend to prefer to do this out of sight and earshot of others and tend to deny that such abuse is taking place—deny to themselves, to the persons they are abusing, and if asked about it by others, to others. After all, emotional abuse, no matter how harsh, is a form of abuse that often can be rather easily hidden. Hiding this abuse to invalidate the abusee's issues and claims of being abused—to **invalidate the abusee**—*is often part of the abuser's process.*

Comments such as, "She thinks I don't love her, but she's

ASK DR. ANGELA
#701: Emotional and Physical Abuse in Relationships, Part One

very wrong," and, "She feels so badly about herself, I just can't get through to her that all this is her imagination," and, "She's making it up because she wants people to think I'm mean and cruel, but you know me, I'm not that kind of person," are heard all the time. How often are such comments:

> *masking something taking place behind closed doors where no one else can see or hear?*

Hidden emotional abuse is painfully common and rarely addressed. Many people just do not get help for something this elusive, something even the reality of which they themselves are frequently forced to question due to invalidation and even attacks on them when they speak of this emotional abuse. This can be the case no matter how intense the abuse is.

In fact, an added level of emotional abuse is a sometimes present and quite convoluted aspect of this abuse—where the person being abused risks "looking crazy" when talking about it, trying to tell anyone it is taking, or has taken, place. In fact, many abusers include in their abuse their *skill* at making the abusee "look crazy."

Being abused in private, either directly or by implication, is not easy to report to others, especially when others may not want to hear, may not believe what they hear, may have contradictory and positive impressions of the abuser, may have a (personal, familial, financial, professional, legal, or other) stake in having the abuser *not* be viewed as the abuser.

ASK DR. ANGELA® SERIES
ASK DR. ANGELA About Intimate and Other Partner Abuse and Violence

EMOTIONAL ABUSE IS SO COMPLEX

The complex matters of intent and consent were introduced in *Chapters 4* and *5*. And of course, their introduction only serves to show how complex these aspects of intimate partner relating are, rather than to simplify these.

Truly, stopping abuse and violence requires more than knowing about the many faces of this abuse and violence; it also takes seeing that the faces themselves are masks for layer upon layer upon layer of intent and consent, confusion about intent and consent, and ***abuse of consent and intent***.

When there is no physical violence, emotional abuse between two adults in a significant other intimate partner relationship is difficult to point to because it typically appears to be taking place with both parties' permission. (If it appears to anyone to be taking place at all, that is). After all, others may say, "They both show up for the abuse event and stick around for it," "The two of them pick on each other, this is just the way they are," and, "There is no physical force compelling one or both to be this way, so how can we call this abuse?"

Certainly, emotional abuse can be mutual; however, quite often it appears mutual when it is not.

Woven throughout emotional abuse is this pervasive and powerful yet all too invisible cruelty:

> **psychological abuse that is frequently**
> **purposefully disguised and denied,**
> **even in its forms of emotional threatening,**
> **manipulation, and extortion**.

ASK DR. ANGELA
#701: Emotional and Physical Abuse in Relationships, Part One

Other terms for this form of abuse in intimate partner relationships indeed include but are not limited to: psychological abuse, mental cruelty, "gas lighting," and quite often the slang description: "mind-f---ing."

NOTHING CAN CAPTURE THE ACTUAL NATURE OF EMOTIONAL ABUSE

Emotional abuse can be an inconvenience, or a problem of sorts. Some emotional abuse can be a serious problem, sometimes quite dangerous, something quite damaging.

So many have endured lives full of emotional abuse, and so many have endured this abuse against the backdrop of physical abuse. So many have accommodated themselves to the reality that they will either continue to be abused, or continue to experience the damaging, harmful effects of this emotional abuse.

The trauma of being severely abused is profound. The trauma of being severely emotionally abused is profound yet all too frequently continuously invalidated. This trauma does not simply evaporate. This trauma requires ongoing attention and care….

ASK DR. ANGELA® SERIES
ASK DR. ANGELA About Intimate and Other Partner Abuse and Violence

ASK DR. ANGELA
#701: Emotional and Physical Abuse in Relationships, Part One

Now, let's continue to look ever more closely at the nature of emotional and physical abuse among intimate and other partners. This abuse affects, harms, damages so many lives. Much of this abuse is not understood, and is not seen for what it is, and not seen as it is developing. … Next see Parts Two, Three, and Four of this set:

ASK DR. ANGELA

About Abuse and Violence

Book #702:
Emotional and Physical Abuse
In Relationships,
<u>Part Two</u>

Book #703:
Emotional and Physical Abuse
In Relationships,
<u>Part Three</u>

Book #704:
Emotional and Physical Abuse
In Relationships,
<u>Part Four</u>

See
www.AskDrAngela.Help
www.DrAngela.com
www.Amazon.com

ASK DR. ANGELA® SERIES
ASK DR. ANGELA About Intimate and Other Partner Abuse and Violence

ASK DR. ANGELA
#701: Emotional and Physical
Abuse in Relationships, Part One

APPENDICES

ASK DR. ANGELA® SERIES
ASK DR. ANGELA About Intimate and Other Partner
Abuse and Violence

ASK DR. ANGELA
#701: Emotional and Physical Abuse in Relationships, Part One

BOOKLIST AND RECOMMENDED READING
See the...
KEYS TO CONSCIOUSNESS AND SURVIVAL SERIES
by Dr. Angela Brownemiller:
****

Volume 9
Navigating Life's Stuff –Dynamics of Personal Change, Book Two
Keys to Consciously Moving Through Our Processes and Their Patterns
****

Volume 8
Navigating Life's Stuff –Dynamics of Personal Change, Book One
Keys to Navigating Our Patterns and Their Processes
****

Volume 7
The Go Conscious Process:
Steps and Practices for Heightening Conscious Awareness,
Shifts, Transmigrations of Focus,
LEAPS OF SELF
****

Volume 6
Overriding the Extinction Scenario, Part Two:
Raising the Bar on the Evolution of the Human Species
****

Volume 5
Overriding the Extinction Scenario, Part One:
Detecting the Bar on the Evolution of the Human Species
****

Volume 4
How to Die and Survive:
Interdimensional Psychology, Consciousness,
and Survival: Concepts for Living and Dying
****

Volume 3
Unveiling the Hidden Instinct:
Understanding Our Interdimensional Survival Awareness
****

Volume 2
Keys to Self: Your Next Steps to YOU
****

Volume 1
Keys to Personal Discovery:
Primer for Life's Minor and Major Challenges and Passages

See next page for additional recommended reading → → →

ASK DR. ANGELA® SERIES
ASK DR. ANGELA About Intimate and Other Partner Abuse and Violence

BOOKLIST AND RECOMMENDED READING
Continued....

VIOLENCE AND ABUSE IN SOCIETY
(four volumes)
Editor, Angela Browne-Miller

INTERNATIONAL COLLECTION ON ADDICTIONS
(four volumes)
Angela Browne-Miller

SEE ALSO...
—

THE BLOODWIN CODE
Episode Books: 1, 2, 3, 4
Dr. Angela Brownemiller

—

Transcending Addiction
Dr. Angela Brownemiller

Seeing The Hidden Face Of Addiction
Dr. Angela Brownemiller

—

Gestalting Addiction
Dr. Angela Brownemiller

Note:
These books should be listed on Amazon.com and numerous other book distributor websites. If not finding these books on these sites and or in book stores, request that these on-ground and or online bookstores order these books, and or contact us at www.DrAngela.com or the author, Dr. Angela Brownemiller., through this website Check also under last name, Browne-Miller. Thank you.

ASK DR. ANGELA
#701: Emotional and Physical
Abuse in Relationships, Part One

ABOUT
THE REAL DR. ANGELA® --
ASK DR. ANGELA ® ABOUT DR. ANGELA®

Some of you have written me asking whether I am various other persons also referring to themselves as *Dr. Angela* and *Ask Dr. Angela*. Thank you for asking.

Let me be clear here. While many people carry the name "Angela" and use that name in various ways, I am the person who holds the trademarks for: *Dr. Angela*® and *Doctor Angela*® and the twitter names: *@DrAngela* and *@AskDrAngela*, and other related addresses and names.

I am an expert in several different fields, including but not limited to: health and wellness, mental health, emotional issues, social-psychological issues, drug and non-drug addiction, emotional and physical abuse and violence, domestic violence, professional and financial abuse, trauma and PTSD, also career and personal development, learning and creativity, and some of my additional favorite topics: the human mind, human consciousness, and human spirit.

To answer some specific questions coming in regarding other persons' work under, and their use of, names such as Dr. Angela and Ask Dr. Angela, let me be clear here: I am neither

ASK DR. ANGELA® SERIES
ASK DR. ANGELA About Intimate and Other Partner Abuse and Violence

an OB/GYN nor a minister, and in no way endorse or not endorse their services simply because they are using the name, Dr. Angela and Ask Dr. Angela. Please always check the credentials and the specific fields of training of persons offering advice and treatment in fields not their own.

My work stands on its own. I have developed extensive national and international expertise over several decades, and written over seventy books on my work, also have four graduate degrees from UC Berkeley including two PhDs, and served as a National Institute on Mental Health Post Doctoral Fellow.

Anyone offering advice in areas I work including but not limited to emotional, behavioral, social, also addiction, abuse, and relationship issues, is not speaking for me or my trademark, Dr. Angela®, and is not communicating with me via any of my contact forms, and or by my *ASK DR. ANGELA®* and or *DR. ANGELA®* functions.

Thank you,
Dr. Angela Brownemiller
DrAngela.com
AskDrAngela.Help

ASK DR. ANGELA
#701: Emotional and Physical
Abuse in Relationships, Part One

ABOUT THE AUTHOR
Dr. Angela Brownemiller
Dr. Angela®

Dr. Angela Brownemiller, also known as Dr. Angela®, is an author, journalist, social thinker, clinician, psychotherapist, trainer, and speaker. The views of Angela Brownemiller are centered on the great potential of the Human mind, heart, and soul, and on the rights of all of us, who and whatever we are (or think we are). Angela Brownemiller views the Human consciousness as a wealth of opportunity for exploration, insight, knowledge — and survival. For more information on her work,
ASK DR. ANGELA, and see DrAngela.com.

The works of Angela Brownemiller are brought to you by:
METATERRA® PUBLICATIONS
(and numerous other publishers, see Amazon.com).

For copies of this and other books by this author,
see Amazon.com

To take part in our events and workshops,
and for personal consultations
in person, online, or by telephone,
contact us at
DrAngela.com

ASK DR. ANGELA® SERIES
ASK DR. ANGELA About Intimate and Other Partner
Abuse and Violence

ASK DR. ANGELA
#701: Emotional and Physical
Abuse in Relationships, Part One

GET THE TRUTH ABOUT ADDICTION
Life-changing insights into the reality of patterns, habits, addictions, and obsessions in our lives and minds.

Now in powerfully narrated AUDIOBOOK as well as PAPERBACK and EBOOK forms!

SEEING THE HIDDEN FACE OF ADDICTION

Detecting and Confronting This Invasive Presence

Dr. Angela Brownemiller

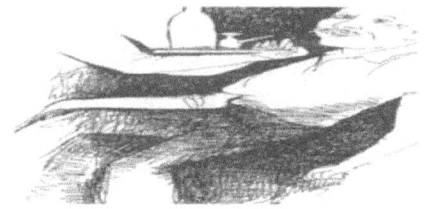

SEEING THE HIDDEN FACE OF ADDICTION
can be found on Amazon.com
and at http://www.DrAngela.com

ASK DR. ANGELA® SERIES
ASK DR. ANGELA About Intimate and Other Partner Abuse and Violence

ASK DR. ANGELA
#701: Emotional and Physical
Abuse in Relationships, Part One

Can we better understand the journeys we travel through in our lives? Can we detect and work with the patterns and processes we are forming, living within, and moving through? How much can we see about the patterns we form, and sometimes feel we cannot change, are caught in? How do we sensitize ourselves to the patterning processes we are engaged in? Find your way through the maze of life. See:

NAVIGATING LIFE'S STUFF:
DYNAMICS OF PERSONAL CHANGE, BOOK ONE
Seeing Our Processes and Their Patterns

NAVIGATING LIFE'S STUFF:
DYNAMICS OF PERSONAL CHANGE, BOOK TWO
Keys to Consciously Moving Through
Our Passages and Their Patterns

Now in Paperback, Audiobook, and Ebook forms.
Find these and other books by Dr. Angela Brownemiller on
Amazon.com and at DrAngela.com....

ASK DR. ANGELA® SERIES
ASK DR. ANGELA About Intimate and Other Partner
Abuse and Violence

See the
ASK DR. ANGELA SERIES

A deep look at ourselves,
our minds, our brains, our lives.

See
AskDrAngela.help
And
DrAngela.com

For list of books
(Paperbacks, Audiobooks, Ebooks),
also workshops, and consult opportunities, in this
ASK DR. ANGELA SERIES
By Angela Brownemiller.
DrAngela.com
Amazon.com

ASK DR. ANGELA
#701: Emotional and Physical
Abuse in Relationships, Part One

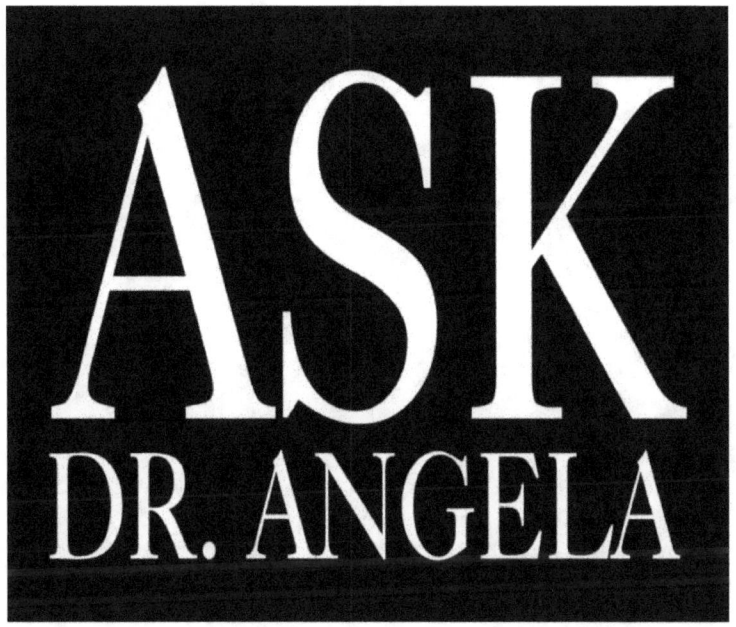